BULOW HAMMOCK

DAVID RAINS WALLACE

BULOW HAMMOCK

Mind in a Forest

SIERRA CLUB BOOKS   SAN FRANCISCO

*The Sierra Club, founded in 1892 by John Muir, has devoted itself
to the study and protection of the earth's scenic and ecological resources—
mountains, wetlands, woodlands, wild shores and rivers, deserts and plains.
The publishing program of the Sierra Club offers books to the public
as a nonprofit educational service in the hope that they may enlarge
the public's understanding of the Club's basic concerns. The point of view expressed
in each book, however, does not necessarily represent that of the Club.
The Sierra Club has some sixty chapters coast to coast, in Canada, Hawaii,
and Alaska. For information about how you may participate in its programs to
preserve wilderness and the quality of life, please address inquiries
to Sierra Club, 730 Polk Street, San Francisco, CA 94109.*

*Library of Congress Cataloging-in-Publication Data
Wallace, David Rains, 1945–
Bulow Hammock: mind in a forest.
Bibliography: p.
1. Natural history—Florida—Bulow Hammock.
2. Bulow Hammock (Fla.) 3. Evolution. I. Title.
QH105.F6W35 1989   508.759'21   88-24009
ISBN 0-87156-676-1*

*Production by Felicity Gorden
Jacket design by Paul Bacon
Book design by Abigail Johnston*

*Printed in the United States of America
10 9 8 7 6 5 4 3 2 1*

TO SARAH G. AND ROBIN C.

Contents

"...when I awoke at midnight, not knowing
where I was, I could not be sure at first
who I was..."
—Proust, *Swann's Way*

BULOW HAMMOCK

The Green Tunnel

THE THING that first struck me about Bulow Hammock is the hardest to describe: the smell. Hammocks are woodlands (the name refers to hardwood groves that punctuate the more open marshes and pine woods of Florida, and may derive from Indian words for "shady place," "garden place," or "floating plants"), but Bulow Hammock didn't smell like any woodlands I knew. I was used to the brisk, humus-and-chlorophyll tang of New England woods with their associations of uplifting weekend hikes. The hammock was different.

I must have been about nine years old when I encountered the hammock, so I didn't articulate any of this. Yet I clearly remember my sensations on stepping out of my parents' car into the shade of the magnolias and cabbage palmettoes. I was fascinated but daunted. The Connecticut woods I'd played in had been inviting, welcoming. The hammock was . . . seductive. It smelled sweet, a perfumey sweetness that reminded me of the hotel lobbies and cocktail lounges I'd occasionally been in with my parents.

Smells are hard to describe because we can't really remember them as we do sights and sounds, we can only recognize them. Smells lie deeper than our remembering, thinking neocortex, in the olfactory lobe we inherited from the early vertebrates. Yet smells are related to thought in profound ways because our nocturnal ancestors, the early mammals, lived by smell. The human ability to relate present to past and future may stem from their scent-tracking of food, an activity which takes place in time as well as space, unlike a hawk's immediate striking on sight, and thus implies planning. The curious resonance the olfactory senses have in memory, as when Proust tasted an epoch in a teacake, suggests that we have a great deal to learn from them.

Complex smells are the hardest to describe. Bulow Hammock smelled stranger than liquor and perfume. It smelled intricately spicy, with a sweetness not so much of flowers as of aromatic bark and leaves. There also was an air of decay in the sweetness; not the rich, sleepy, somewhat bitter decay of New England woods, but more of a nervous, sour atmosphere. When I scraped my foot over fallen leaves on the ground, I didn't uncover the soft brown dirt I was used to, but white sand and a network of fine, blackish roots like the hair of a buried animal. The sand was part of the smell too, a dusty, siliceous undertone to the spice and decay.

There was something dangerous about the smell, something inhibiting to my nine-year-old mind. I didn't want to rush into the hammock as I'd have wanted to rush into an unfamiliar Connecticut woodland. It wasn't that the hammock seemed ugly or repellent—on the contrary. The seductiveness was part of the inhibition. Perhaps it was just that the hammock was *so* unfamiliar. It's easy to read things into childhood memories. But the smell was powerful.

Society is suspicious of wild places because it fears a turning away from human solidarity toward a spurious, sentimental freedom. It is interesting, in this regard, to recall how *little* of freedom there was in my first perception of Bulow Hammock, how little of the unfettered feeling I got in sand dunes, hill meadows, pine woods or other open places that promised release from streets and classrooms. I wonder if the hammock inhibited me because there was more of humanity about it than a dune, meadow, or pine forest has; not of humanity in the sense of society and civilization, which (however irrationally, given the history of civilization) we associate with safety, but of animal humanity, of the walking primate that has spent most of its evolution in warm places like Florida: spicy, moldy, sandy places. Perhaps it wasn't the strangeness of the hammock that made it seem dangerously seductive, but a certain familiarity. It is, after all, dangerous to be human.

We'd come to Florida to visit my father's mother, who had a retirement cottage in Ormond-by-the-Sea, an early geriatric enclave complete with shuffleboard court (which, three decades later, has become somebody's driveway). On the drive south, we passed another stretch of coastal hammock that was being burned and bulldozed during some kind of road construction involving sweaty convicts in gray twill. There'd been something very malignant-looking about that stretch of charred palmetto. Blackened fronds had thrust at the sky like fire-sharpened spears. As though to heighten the effect, someone had erected a doll's head, also charred, on a crooked stick.

I couldn't have looked at this scene for more than a few seconds, but it made a big impression. At nine, I had no very firm grasp of its rational implications, of the likelihood that the head had been stuck up there by some whimsically ghoulish convict who'd found it while grubbing in the brush. I must have been aware of that likelihood, but other things seemed possible: that it was a real head, a baby's or a monkey's; that it manifested an unknown savage world in the uncut hammock farther from the road, of which there was a lot more in Florida then. The southern landscape threw the human

3

and wild together more than the northern. I remember a great loneliness in it, brown fields of broomsedge reaching almost to the horizon, and unpainted shacks against ragged woods over which circled vultures in numbers out of proportion to the vacancy beneath them. The blackwater swamps that the road periodically passed over seemed cheerful in comparison, albeit dangerous.

Of course, my response to the road construction—fire, sticks, head, uncut green wall in the distance—was an educated one, as was my response to Bulow Hammock's smell. It would be banal to assert that the smell awakened atavistic race memories of life in the jungle. We'd been getting our first taste of human evolution in my fourth grade class, and I'd found *that* pretty spicy, all those skeletons and hairy people: Piltdown Man (we must have been the last class to learn about Piltdown Man, since the hoax was discovered around that year), Java Man, Peking Man. A normally bloodthirsty fourth-grader, I'd thrilled to learn that Peking Man had scooped out and probably eaten the brains of other Peking men. I'd seen the "green hell" jungle movies of the early 1950s: Charlton Heston in *The Naked Jungle,* Jeff Chandler in *Green Fire.* I had a whole set of cultural preconceptions ready for Bulow Hammock.

Yet banality is a kind of fossilized reality, the bones of insights buried in the silt of intellectual fashion. I wouldn't dismiss my nine-year-old perceptions just because they were culturally conditioned. Classrooms and movie theaters teach little about smell, for one thing, and, sophisticated as they are, they still share with nine-year-olds a descent from spicy, moldy, sandy places. We don't know enough about that descent to dismiss anything. Fire, sticks, head, and green wall have been at the center of things for most of human experience, and they still are, in a sense, although the green wall may have receded.

A green wall is what Bulow Hammock seemed as my father drove down the low sand road leading into it, or rather a green arch, a tunnel. Its surfaces seemed much more solid than the crumbly coquina of the nineteenth-century sugar plantation ruins we had come to the hammock to see. The mill was roofless while the hammock enclosed us completely, from its ground-hugging coontie, dog hobble, and saw palmetto to its undergrowth of bayberry, hornbeam, and dahoon to its canopy of live oak, red bay, magnolia and cabbage palmetto. Glimpses of the hammock interior lacked perspective: they had the wavery, spotty aspect of underwater things. The plant forms were too eccentric for geometry—palm, spike, spray, corkscrew, club, plume, lace, spiral. It was beautiful, but the intricacy was like the complexity of smell. It inhibited. Its seductiveness was also a warning because it hinted at passionate entanglement more than freedom or tranquillity.

I followed my parents around the sugar mill ruins like a good little boy. The Seminoles had burned the plantation in 1835: that was interesting. There were displays of implements found in the ruins, and a brochure about the plantation's history. There wasn't any explanation of the hammock. There may have been signs identifying birds or plants, but if there were, they did little to elucidate the fearful seductiveness of the place, a seductiveness to which the adult world seemed curiously immune. But then, children are used to being surrounded by powerful, unexplained seductions.

I never did venture into the hammock as a child, although I was wandering miles through the Connecticut woods. I don't recall going more than a few yards even into the barrier island scrub that grew behind my grandmother's cottage in the fifties, before the Ormond Mall was built. The mailman had put his hand into a pile of leaves (trusting children, we didn't ask why) and withdrawn it with a coral snake attached to the skin between his fingers. Coral snakes, Grandmother told my sister and me, had to hold and chew their victims to inject their almost invariably fatal poison.

Grandmother wasn't a snake-hater: her deepest antipathies were for the British royal family (her father was Irish) and J. Edgar Hoover (her former employer). She was more passionate in her opinions than most grandmothers, always applauding when Harry Truman appeared in movie newsreels whether or not anybody else did. Perhaps because of this, her dictums had considerable authority, and we weren't about to put our hands in any dead leaves, or our feet. There were poisonous copperheads in the Connecticut woods, of course, but they didn't chew on you. We contented ourselves with watching big toads eat little toads in her backyard.

The Beach

OF COURSE, Florida wasn't all unnerving jungle: the hammock and scrub were just a background to water and light. My first sight of Florida was on awakening at dawn in my parents' car driving down A1A between the dunes, covered with silvery blue sea oats and saw palmettoes, and the opalescent beach. There were few structures on the dunes then, no high-rises, and it seemed the most untroubled place in the world, soft as a dream in pastels of pink, beige, and turquoise.

A flock of pelicans appeared, soaring level with the car. I could see their plumage in surprising detail: the white head feathers shading to yellow in front, blue eyes ringed with pink skin, a chestnut stripe down the back of the neck. They were the biggest wild birds I'd ever seen close up, but they didn't seem ungainly or intimidating. Their soft colors and the peculiar stillness they manifested as they glided beside the car made them seem part of the hospitality of the place, a southern hospitality more convincing to me, even in material-istic childhood, than the billboards hawking fried chicken and homemade biscuits.

I'd never seen colors like the ones in Florida. It was like a huge ice cream sundae for which I never lost appetite, the eastern horizon heaped with clouds of purple, vermilion, auburn, even green. The clouds seemed to change color every time I turned around, and reflected a similar if slightly diluted brilliance onto water so warm, so unlike the dank rubbery brine of Long Island Sound, that I could stay in it as long as I liked. I didn't get tired of it even after I drifted out over my head and came near to drowning myself, and my sister too, before a passing adult waded out to extract us.

Even the sand was brightly colored, especially where it met the water. Millions of tiny coquina shells covered it with pink, blue, violet, yellow, and orange, and if I watched carefully I could see thousands of live coquinas suddenly join the dead ones as surf washed the little bivalves from their burrows and rolled them around. When the wave had receded, each coquina protruded a miniscule, transparent foot, upended itself, and chugged back into the sand, the thousands disappearing as abruptly as they had appeared.

Other sleight-of-hand experts lived farther from the water. Ghost crabs were the same off-white as the sand, so they didn't need to pop out of burrows to appear out of nowhere: they could do it simply by moving. Electric-azure and yellow six-lined race runner lizards should have been more conspicuous, but they weren't. They could run faster than the eye could follow, and their colors matched the blue of saw palmetto and the yellow of beach marigold. Farther into the scrub were slender green anole lizards that could turn brown or gray when they chose to mimic bark instead of leaves, and sand skinks with only a faint, coppery sheen to distinguish them from the ground litter.

I suppose the Florida seashore struck me as hospitable because it seemed childish, like me: soft and smooth, full of bright, timid little things, a nursery of life like the Paleozoic seas whose bright colors and odd shapes attracted me in illustrated evolution books. It abetted longings for some kind of self-sufficient, prehuman life free from the perpendicular demands of society. When I spent all afternoon on the warm beach, it seemed desirable to live in a sand burrow, sit at its mouth, watch the terns and pelicans circling, and be content with that, no siblings, parents, teachers; just the odd lizard, the sandpipers running before the surf.

Of course, such longings are regressive. Even a ghost crab lives in a social milieu, beset with the territorial demands of other ghost crabs. A search for untroubled self-sufficiency wouldn't even end with the amoeba, since even it must live with other amoebas. I suppose I'd have become autistic if I'd realized those longings; still, we may lose something, some umbilical connection to the biosphere as a whole, if we don't have them. A longing for complete self-sufficiency is almost the same as a longing for complete integration, for a solitude so perfect it is not lonely.

I continued to associate Florida with ease and safety after I grew up. (I imagine a lot of my generation grew up doing so.) My family kept the cottage after Grandmother died, and I'd go there when I was feeling anxious or at loose ends. Once, when feeling particularly so, I drove all the way from New York in thirty-six straight hours: by the time I reached the Florida border, a thunderstorm on the horizon looked like a cosmic gateway into refuge, purple lightning thumping down from black sky in the best science-fiction time-warp manner.

At first I'd just lie on the beach, but later I began taking trips inland to wild places. Even those had a kind of holiday atmosphere. Despite a conventional reputation for gloom, most southern swamps and forests are rather light and airy — pine savannas, wet prairies, saw grass and sphagnum marshes. Even bald cypress swamps have a lot of sparkle, since the cypresses are small-leaved conifers and lose their leaves entirely in the gloomier times of year. One travels through them in a canoe, certainly one of the more easeful modes of travel — on still water, at least.

Florida became even more hospitable, in a sense, as I grew older and freeways replaced the old two-lane highways. The unpainted shacks, road gangs and circling vultures receded, taking with them the menace and desolation I'd sensed as a child. Compared to the raw strip developments and flag-flapping theme parks that sprouted in their place, the old Spanish moss and silvery board South began to seem harmonious, rational. Even the hibiscus and crabgrass of Grandmother's 1950s retirement tract, already getting run-down, and populated in the 1980s by as many biker types as retirees, seemed almost antebellum when set against the neo-Pompeiian beach condominiums across Highway A1A.

The Spiders

I WENT BACK to the Bulow ruins a few times during various Florida trips. It was surprising how little they changed despite the Daytona area's rampant urbanization. Each time I found the same bumpy sand road and green tunnel. Even the trees didn't seem to get bigger. The same Bermuda grass lawn led to Bulow Creek and its palmettoes and marshes; the same resurrection ferns, maiden cane, and bromeliads festooned the gray coquina walls. The same smell struck me when I got out of the car.

I still never went far into the hammock that stretched southward. It didn't seem like much compared to the Okefenokee Swamp or Ocala National Forest, and it was private property. I imagined tennis courts and golf courses would soon obliterate it, as the Ormond Mall had obliterated the scrub behind my grandmother's house and "Tomoka View," "Tomoka Oaks," "North Forty," and "The Trails" had obliterated the hammock along the Tomoka River where I'd seen my first wild alligator while riding on Captain Frank's Jungle Cruise. I wasn't conscious of the uneasiness I'd felt as a child. The hammock just didn't seem very noticeable.

Then I saw an article in the Daytona paper during a visit in the early 1980s. A corporation had been trying to develop the hammock for homes, but because it was one of the last tatters of forest on the East Coast, there'd been active opposition. Now the state was going to buy thousands of acres of the hammock from the corporation as a park. The paper got semi-lyrical about the hammock: it had been wilderness since the Seminoles burned the plantation; there were deer, bobcats, maybe even the odd bear or Florida panther (although this last seemed unlikely since the hammock was cut off from inland by I-95).

I was getting a little bored with lying on the beach, canoeing in the Tomoka estuary, and pulling weeds in my grandmother's yard. Ever the nonconformist, she had covered it with quartz pebbles instead of the traditional turf. It was a nice idea, like having a Zen garden, but the sand kept working its way up through the pebbles along with wiry little sandburs and wild poinsettias. We who came to lounge on lawn chairs ended up stooped over the pebbles with trowels, which would have gratified my grandmother, who liked seeing people usefully employed.

One morning when it was too windy for the beach (it was November), I drove past the miles of increasingly affluent homes that had replaced the barrier island scrub north of my grandmother's subdivision, and crossed the Halifax River. Things still hadn't changed noticeably up there. The state highway running east from coastal A1A looked just as it had thirty years before—a drawbridge, salt marshes, a curve with big old faded farmhouses on a knoll, more marsh, a fishing bridge over Bulow Creek, a long straight stretch under spreading live oaks. The bumpy sand road was there, and the smell, spicy and seductive.

There still weren't any paths into the hammock. A weedy track ended in an ancient garbage dump, and some developer's bulldozings were evident, but they were already overgrown with dog fennel, Devil's walkingstick, and longleaf pine seedlings. I walked down another weedy track, and when that ended in head-high saw grass and black mud, I walked down another, which eventually led me into the mature woods where walking was easier.

I began to get excited. The place *was* wild. Even though it was an hour's drive from the world's most disgusting beach, as Daytona Beach is affectionately called, its density gave it integrity and presence. The live oaks and swamp hickories were as big as any I'd seen. The wind in their branches was the only sound.

The farther I got in, the more I began to wonder about getting out. I was pretty sure I could recall the way, but not absolutely sure. It's very hard to be sure about directions in a level, closed-canopy woodland. Of course, if I forgot, I could simply walk north until I hit the sand road, but it was getting late. It might get dark. The park would be closed, and I'd have to ask the ranger to let me out. I didn't have a flashlight, and although poisonous snakes were very unlikely to be encountered, they were there. My excitement skewed slightly. I felt a prickle of ice water in the spine.

Although it was fall, the hammock was full of mosquitoes and ticks (and chiggers, as I realized later when their bites started itching). There were vast numbers of orb weaver spiders, at least one to every bush. I kept walking into the webs, and into the spiders: huge yellow ones, six inches across, with hairy legs; pink and green ones that looked like flower buds; gold and white ones with spine-covered abdomens. One of the huge ones (called a golden silk spider) had caught a young anole lizard in its web, had wrapped it in silk, and was eating the flesh of the head. The lizard's white skull gleamed strangely from the gray web.

Warblers and titmice fussed in the canopy, a woodpecker

drummed in the distance. Unseen things rustled in the leaves and underbrush. It's normal to feel that much life is hidden in wild places, but the hammock seemed to be carrying this to extremes. The thin leaf litter was disturbed everywhere by burrowings, rootings and scratchings. Little paths honey-combed the saw palmetto scrub; tree trunks swelled to but-tress roots that formed cryptic recesses; every fallen log seem-ed hollow, eaten through by termites and beetles, inhabited by God knew what.

As I passed a hop hornbeam sapling that had broken off at eye level, I glanced into the cavity. A little green tree frog huddled there, its eyes and back spangled with gold, like a bit of hidden treasure. It flinched when I touched it, but stayed put, as though preferring its shelter, even when dis-covered, to the hammock at large.

I didn't get far into the hammock that day. I spent a lot of time memorizing such landmarks as a level, evergreen forest provides, making little signs for myself out of fallen palmetto fronds. A stiff evening breeze arose, tossing the palmettoes and clattering the hardwoods. It's impressive, when one is in the mood to notice such things, how much a breeze can bend a tree. I saw myself lying beneath a fallen branch, my skull gleaming like the anole's. When I turned back, it was a relief.

The Lost One

AS A CHILD, I often got lost in the woods because I'd rush in without a thought of finding my way out. Search parties never were required, but I spent many afternoons circling distractedly in swampy second growth. This approach to exploration climaxed in college when some friends and I climbed Mount Washington in New Hampshire without packs, maps, food, or any other equipment except summer jackets. I don't recall feeling too worried when, as we got above timberline, it started to get dark and snow, but I was glad, and surprised, when we came to the hostel halfway up the mountain. Seeing the grave monuments that dot the peak did make me a little wiser the next day.

Such memories came back as I groped my way through Bulow Hammock. It was embarrassing. I had travelled, written books, but I quailed before this . . . thicket. If I could still get lost with my middle-aged knowledge, it reflected on the quality of the knowledge. I had accumulated a lot of it, but like most accumulations, it never seemed quite enough. After the energy and desire of learning about something were spent, I'd feel a void within my expanded horizons that could only be filled, it seemed, with more knowledge, as though the thrill of discovery was as psychologically addicting as

15

marijuana. Sometimes I felt like a balloon, getting thinner-skinned as I expanded until some weak point would give way and I'd burst or subside in a spluttering of hot air.

It wasn't an unusual predicament—in fact, it was typical: to mature, achieve, and then be reduced to bewilderment by an unresolved past. That my latest bewilderment concerned a patch of semitropical forest seemed all the more typical, since that was where humans come from. I certainly wasn't the first to stand in bewilderment before a green wall. Florida hammocks have a long history of bewilderment, beginning with Ponce de León in 1513, although Ponce's experience is as much myth as history. He is supposed to have struggled through the hammocks looking for the fountain of youth, but his expedition's accounts mention only Indian hostilities and navigational problems.

Bulow Hammock itself was the site of one of the more articulate, indeed vociferous, bewilderments in American history. In 1831, a middle-aged John James Audubon spent a few weeks at the Bulow sugar plantation, then a thriving enterprise with a small army of slaves tending thousands of acres of indigo and cotton as well as sugar cane. Audubon spoke highly of his wealthy host's library and table, but much less so of the surrounding wilderness. In fact, he seems to have hated almost every minute he spent in it, which is odd considering his enthusiasm for the wilds of Ohio and Louisiana.

"I have been deceived most shamefully about the Floridas," he wrote. "Scarcely a bird is to be seen, and those of the most common sorts . . . I felt unquiet, too, in this singular scene, as if I were almost upon the verge of creation where realities were tapering off into nothing. The general wilderness, the eternal labyrinth of waters and marshes, interlocked and apparently never ending; the whole surrounded by interminable swamp—all these things have a tendency to depress my spirits."

A few days after Christmas, Audubon set off from the plantation house at what was then called "Bulow Ville" to do some
collecting for *Birds of America*. In a boat with "three white
men," including his twenty-six-year-old host, John Bulow, and
six black "hands," he floated down Bulow Creek to the Halifax
River, where he was "anxious to kill some twenty-five brown
pelicans." After staying overnight near the river's mouth, the
party found the pelicans, but the slave who loaded Audubon's
second gun put the powder in after the shot, so the birds
escaped. Then the tide went out, and their boat was stranded
in mud some three thousand yards from shore. They passed
an uncomfortable night under a cold northeast wind.

In the morning, they decided to push the boat through
the mud to some trees five or six hundred yards away. This
took them two and a half hours, and two of the "hands" col-
lapsed, "fell down in the marsh as senseless as torpidity ever
rendered an alligator or snake: and had we, *the white men*,
not been there, they certainly would have died." They built
a fire and revived the slaves with hot tea, then set off through
a "head-high salt marsh" to look for open water. When they
found it, "our spirits rose to such a pitch that we in fun set
fire to the salt marsh: crack, crack, crack! went the reeds with
rapid blaze."

Elation was premature: they soon ran aground again. The
"three white men" eventually had to walk back along the
beach, not a romantic pursuit in those days, "through sand
that sent our feet back six inches at every step, until we
reached the landing place of J. J. Bulow . . . as we saw the large
house opening to view across his immense plantation, I anticipated a good dinner with as much pleasure as I ever
experienced."

Audubon was eloquent about his discomfort at "wading
through the swamps and salt marshes or scrambling through

the vilest thickets of scrubby live oaks and palmettoes that appear to have been created for no other purpose than to punish us for our sins," but he wrote less colorfully about actually getting lost. "The best woodsmen are not infrequently bewildered for a while," he cautiously observed, "and I well remember that such an occurrence happened to myself at a time when I had imprudently ventured to pursue a wounded quadruped that led me some distance from the track." Audubon's fame and fortune rested to some extent on his reputation as an "American woodsman," so his reticence on a potential embarrassment is understandable. In fact, it's praiseworthy that he mentioned it, in a sketch entitled "The Lost One" in his *Ornithological Biography.*

The lost one isn't Audubon, but a woodcutter living near the St. Johns River, who sets out one foggy morning to fell ship timber in a live oak hammock but never gets there. "To his alarm, at the moment the fog dispersed, he saw the sun at its meridian height, and could not recognize a single object around him . . . Time passed, and the sun headed his course: he saw it gradually descend to the west; but all around him continued as if enveloped in mystery. The huge gray trees spread their giant boughs over him, the rank grass extended on all sides, not a living being crossed his path, all was silent and still, and the scene was like a dull and dreary drama of the land of oblivion."

The woodcutter wanders forty days, eating grass, a tortoise, a raccoon, palm hearts, snakes, frogs, but steadily gets weaker until he stumbles on a boating party which rescues him, thirty-eight miles from his starting place. "The condition of a man lost in the woods," Audubon concluded, "is one of the most perplexing that could be imagined by a person who has not himself been in a like predicament. Every object he sees, he at first thinks he recognizes, and while his whole mind is bent on searching for more that may gradually lead to his extrication, he goes on committing greater errors the farther he proceeds."

Audubon got out of Florida pretty quickly, as did another bewildered explorer thirty-eight years later. John Muir had long dreamed of palmettoes and magnolias, but when he set out to walk from Fernandina on Florida's northeast coast to Cedar Key on the west in 1869, he found himself virtually restricted to a railroad embankment by swamps, thickets, and fear of alligators and "robber negroes." When he ventured from the right-of-way, he became "tangled in a labyrinth of armed vines like a fly in a spider web . . . a traveller in open woods can form no idea of the crooked and strange difficulties of pathless locomotion in these thorny, watery southern tangles." He made it across the state, but then spent three months on his back with malaria, and finally caught the next boat for Cuba and California.

The educated flounderings of our greatest naturalists compare oddly with stories of animals and ignorant people, such as Eugene Marais tells in *The Soul of the Ape:* the mare that walked straight across a trackless desert for six days to return to the camp where she was usually kept; the fourteen-year-old Bushman who walked forty miles across a mountain range he'd never been in before to get home. When asked how he'd accomplished this, he said: "I did not know where my home was. I ran away because I wanted to go home." Audubon and Muir always reached their destinations, but it would be hard to imagine even those great woodsmen heading so unerringly for an unknown location.

Animals and ignorant people can get lost as well as educated ones: they can wander off aimlessly and end up in the wrong place. Yet animals may be quite calm even when they *are* lost, miles from their accustomed places, while educated humans often get hysterical when they *aren't* lost, when they're only a grove of trees or a hilltop away from their destination. Education seems to make getting lost more fearful, not less.

Our fear of getting lost has extended beyond geography. Almost every square mile of the world has been mapped in detail, but a sense of misplacement and bewilderment grows, and with reason. In an evolutionary sense, we are misplaced from the ecological niche for which biology prepared us. We're so misplaced that we've only just realized we ever had an ecological niche, that we didn't start out living all over the planet as Eskimos and Bedouins and Indo-Europeans.

This long-forgotten past now fascinates us, as though we hope it will restore a sense of orientation. We comb Ethiopian and Tanzanian badlands for hominid bones and pursue harried apes around Borneo and Zaire seeking older connections. Yet paleontology and anthropology sometimes seem a little like digging wells on a lakeshore. We marvel as the water trickles into the carefully dug holes, but turn our backs on its source because it seems too big and murky to tap. Our brains haven't changed that much physically from our hominid ancestors', and the planet they perceive has changed little. At one point, the brain was regarded as a tabula rasa at birth, a blankness waiting to be programmed by learning and experience. Now we know that the brains of even newborn organisms are preset to do some complex things. Newborn humans can cling to overhanging branches like monkeys. The unlearned spatial orientation Marais observed in the young Bushman might also be innate in some way. At least, the fact that such orientation seems erased or obscured in educated people suggests an innate origin. Infants lose their branch-gripping reflex before they learn to walk.

Our fear of getting lost in the woods might arise from a psychological dislocation as much as from a geographical one. A brain innately equipped with a self-guiding reflex might panic on finding itself cut off from that reflex. Of course, the idea of a brain panicking, or doing anything on its own, goes against a basic concept of biology: we assume that *organisms* panic, not brains, that the organism is the highest functional unit. This is certainly true in that most of the organism is involved in panic, not just the brain. Yet, when people get lost in the woods, the brain seems to *induce* panic in an organism not immediately threatened, suggesting that the organism is not the solid unit we like to believe it is.

I was sensitive to this notion as I walked in Bulow Hammock, because my brain had been giving my organism a hard time. My small bewilderment in the hammock echoed a big one I'd been experiencing for several years while backpacking in the western mountains. I'd felt safer sleeping out in the woods than in civilization, but disturbing things had started to happen. I'd begun having irrational fits of terror. Dozing in my sleeping bag, or walking along a trail, I'd suddenly experience dizziness, a racing heart, cold sweats. Sometimes if I closed my eyes I'd see bony human faces mouthing incomprehensible words. I went to a doctor, who found nothing wrong physically. I might as well have been possessed by evil spirits.

A young man who'd spent a lot of time in the Monterey backcountry phoned me around that time.

"Do you mind if I ask you something?" he said. "I'd been living up there all summer. It was nice, I felt at home. But then one morning, I woke up covered with sweat. I felt I didn't know where I was, or even *what* I was. Like I was turning into a rock."

"Hm."

"I'd never felt anything like that. I couldn't stay up there afterward. I had to come out for a while. Do you know anything about this?"

"I think I may know what you mean."

"Really? Is this something people know about? I mean, I don't hear them talking about it."

"I've felt something like it."

"Really? In the woods? Then what is it? Do you know?"

"No."

The young man and I seemed to have experienced the "lost one" 's distressing symptoms without even being lost, geographically, at least. After writing some books about them, I thought I knew something about western mountain forests. I wondered how real the knowledge was if my mind could behave so unexpectedly in them. The first time it happened, I'd been sure I was dying. The forest had seemed a "land of oblivion" indeed.

Perhaps I needed to know my mind better before I could get on with understanding the forest. Yet traditional ways of knowing minds had remarkably little to do with forests. Psychiatry could have told me about night sweats, but it would have concerned parents or toilet training rather than trees. I wanted to understand my mind in relation to trees.

It seemed at least a possible aspiration. If my mind was imperfectly related to my entire organism, it was also related to other things, like forests. Organisms exist in ecosystems, after all, and ecosystems shape organisms. Of course, forest life stopped shaping the human brain directly a long time ago. Yet one of the first things psychologists learned about the unconscious brain is that time doesn't exist for it, that childhood memories are as "present" as those of five minutes ago. If the brain retains innate "memories" such as spatial orientation, they also may be timeless, if hidden.

22

I couldn't think of a place where my relationship to forest went back further than Bulow Hammock. It was the only forest I'd known as child and adult. I even had ancestors in swampy southern lowlands. One of them had swum the Pee Dee River escaping a British prison camp during the Revolutionary War. There also were much earlier ancestors, in a sense, because the hammock had tropical aspects, and the human mind evolved in warm, spicy places.

I wondered if I might explore the hammock not only as a home of wild plants and animals but as a connection to my wayward brain. The brain is like forests in being diverse and multilayered. I'd even felt in the western mountains that the old-growth forests might have a kind of consciousness arising from complexity. Like my brain, the hammock was structured hierarchically, with newer, more complex things growing from older ones. Most mysteriously, brain and hammock shared a propensity for mimesis, for producing similarities between different things.

I didn't expect anything conclusive from the experiment. I felt like a medieval man trying to map the universe. We have no mental telescope, and may never. Still, that was no reason for not trying. I wouldn't have to drive hundreds of miles on lousy Forest Service logging roads as I had in the western mountains, and I might wind up farther from the pavement, in a sense.

The Whisk Fern

I WENT BACK to the hammock a few days later. This time I kept going through the spiderwebs until I came to a more open place, a swampy floodplain dotted with big cabbage palmettoes and red cedars. Chest-high swamp ferns grew on the ground or the palmettoes with impartiality. There were also some red maples, the same species that fires up New England in autumn. Their fallen leaves looked incongruous under the palmettoes. Even more incongruously for November, the red maples were about to flower, their deep red buds swelling as their northern conspecifics wouldn't until April.

Despite these simultaneous aspects of New England spring and fall, the swamp looked venerably tropical to me. Palm trees dot swampy watersides, particularly coastal ones, throughout the tropics. The breeze smelled of a black mud one doesn't find in the deepest of temperate swamps, a mud that might have spontaneously generated the swarms of mosquito fish agitating otherwise stagnant pools. Even the ferns were bigger and coarser than temperate ferns. The palmetto fronds seemed too heavy for their trunks and clattered startlingly in the breeze, a sound very unlike the maples' sedate murmurs.

A troop of lesser goldfinches flew down to drink, like a miniature parrot flock in their fussiness and greenish plumage, then shot away. I crossed a rivulet on a palmetto log, of which great numbers lay about (as I could understand from the way wind whipped the standing ones back and forth). When I bent to pass one precariously leaning trunk, my eyes fell on a little plant growing on the palmetto's swollen base.

It was an odd plant, leafless, a spray of wiry green stems with bulbous, pea-size structures at the joints. I'd never seen a living one, but I remembered it from a college biology textbook. It was a whisk fern, which isn't really a fern, and isn't related closely to any common plant alive today. It's much more primitive than ferns, lacking real root structures as well as leaves, and reproducing only in specialized moist environments because the sperm must swim through dew or other surface moisture to reach the egg cells. It's pretty much the same as the plants of 400 million years ago.

Bulow Hammock was even more venerably tropical than I'd thought. Whisk ferns grow only in warm climates today (Hawaii has them too) and probably always have. Life had enough trouble climbing out of water without dealing with frost at the same time. Here was a survivor of the first tropical forest perched gnomelike on a distant descendant.

There were other survivors. In a grassy glade, I came to a plant that resembled a small, trunkless palm. It was coontie, which isn't a palm but a cycad, a group of plants that has lived in the tropics for about a hundred million years longer than palms. I've heard that few insects eat cycads because most modern insects evolved after they did, although I've seen modern-looking caterpillars eating cycad leaves. Most modern insects did evolve along with flowering plants, and cycads aren't flowering plants, but gymnosperms. They bear naked seeds in conelike structures as do their relatives, the conifers.

In keeping with their tropical background, coonties bear much showier cones than pines or firs. Although small and ground-hugging, they sport eggplant-size female cones enclosing coral red seeds as big as Brazil nuts. They look highly edible, whether or not sufficiently primitive creatures exist to eat them. Perhaps their color attracted dinosaurs.

Coonties have trunks, but they are underground, as though the ancient plants are intimidated by the big angiosperms around them and try to keep a low profile. The trunks are also nutritiously starchy, tempting to hard-toothed mammals. Prehistoric cycads were bolder: some had barrel-like trunks on which grew reproductive structures of almost flowerlike showiness.

Palms may be tropical parvenus compared to whisk ferns and coonties, but they still have a respectable lineage. Palmettoes of the genus *Sabal* have existed at least since the dinosaurs died off. Flowering plants in general probably originated in the tropics, perhaps from cycadlike ancestors, although nobody knows, since fossils of the first flowering plants haven't been discovered. New organisms tend to evolve in the tropics, because speciation proceeds faster in warm climates, and much of evolution has consisted of tropical organisms spreading into temperate zones, a process continuing today in the northward migration of opossums and coatis. Even animals that seem basically adapted to cold, such as mammals with their hairiness and warm-bloodedness, probably had tropical origins. The oldest mammal types, including primates, are mainly tropical.

Finding the whisk fern and cycad made me feel I was beginning to get somewhere. Not only had I *found* something which in itself provides a certain sense of orientation, but I'd found evidence of impressive tropical continuity in this thicket beset with freeways and resort communities. It gave me hope of finding something equally ancient and significant in my tangled and beset brain. I went on with renewed confidence, but continued caution, keeping between the open swamp and the denser hardwoods, in a southerly direction toward the hammock's center. The going was easy for a while, the golds and reds of the hickories and sweet gums cheerful to look at.

But going seldom stays easy in a trackless woodland, even in a thicket. The mud got muddier and produced large numbers of tall, fleshy plants that looked like lilies, although they weren't flowering. I was driven increasingly into the hardwoods, which were getting gloomier as evergreen magnolias predominated over deciduous maples and sweet gums. The magnolias posed an intellectual problem as well as a physical one. With their big, glossy leaves and pale, knobby bark, they looked gratifyingly primitive and tropical, but there were problems with this. Magnolias are indeed among the most primitive angiosperms, as indicated by their wood and flowers. Their conelike fruits, from which red seeds protrude, remind one of coontie cones. Unfortunately, magnolia fossils are more common in Greenland than the tropics, and this is not just because of continental drift. Magnolias are mainly temperate zone plants today, the only tropical species growing at high, cool elevations.

Then the demarcation between swamp and hardwoods that I'd been following petered out in a sunken streambed full of snaky roots and black pools and overhung with dense vegetation. There was more swamp to the west, but it was too wet to walk comfortably in. Something was moving around in it, something pretty big. I heard wings, caught a glimpse of something black and white, and rather scaly looking. It was probably just a wood stork, a bird with a naked, wrinkled head, but it seemed macabre among the huge, flowerless lilies.

I'd passed through a sizeable patch of chest-high saw palmetto to get to the swamp in the first place. I decided it was
time to see if I could pass back. I did, without difficulty, but
not without some agitation from my brain. I could feel anxious electrical impulses shooting down my spine toward my
legs and stomach, telling those extremities to get a move on.
I resisted them, trying to be a good integral organism, finding and following my little arrows. It was near sunset when
I got back on the track. I sat on a fallen trunk to see what
creatures might appear, but none did.

The Subtropics

A CLOSE LOOK at the hammock ecosystem tempered my aspirations for brain-forest connections. With its odd assortment of temperate maples and magnolias, tropical palms and cycads, the hammock seemed a slippery sort of entity to connect with, if an entity at all. Some scientists see the miscellaneous aspect of forest species — magnolias living with redwoods in Greenland in one epoch, with palms in Florida in another — as evidence that ecosystems are not really entities but assemblages of organisms living together merely because they happen to share certain requirements. After all, if a cooling climate killed all the palmettoes in Bulow Hammock, the magnolias would remain because they range farther north. Such obvious facts support the conventional view that organisms are the highest entities, the ones worthy of legal and ethical standing. Organisms don't usually survive the loss of an organ as ecosystems survive that of a species.

Yet the comparison may not be entirely fair. When ecosystems lose or acquire species, they usually do so over the span of evolutionary time, and organisms have also been known to lose or acquire organs during that time span, as anybody who has had an appendix out knows. Ecosystems seem pretty sloppy as they wander over the plate tectonic map, shedding and picking up species, but they retain a lot of continuity. Perhaps our geographical way of classifying them is too crude. Bulow Hammock seems neither tropical nor temperate, but a loose amalgam of the two, because it is neither tropical rain forest nor temperate beech-maple forest. Yet parts of the hammock go considerably further into the past than rain forest or beech-maple forest. If whisk ferns and cycads are miscellaneous visitors, they certainly are persistent ones.

To say that the hammock is a miscellaneous assemblage between tropical and temperate because it contains oaks, hickories, blueberries, and pines as well as palms, laurels, bromeliads, and cycads seems uninformative when one considers that forests very like it have existed for as long as, or longer than, tropical rain forests or beech-maple forests. Such a "subtropical" forest covered what are now the deserts and grasslands of mid-latitude Europe, Asia, and North America during most of the past sixty-five million years, until glaciation and dessication squeezed it into a few places like Florida and southeast China. It's easy now to call such remnants "transitional," but if we'd lived fifty million years ago, we might have called the hammock an "integrated" forest between the "extremes" of tropical and temperate.

Our ancestors of fifty million years ago doubtless would have agreed with such a positive estimation of the hammock, because they inhabited ecosystems very like it. We associate our primate antecedents with high rain forest such as apes and monkeys inhabit today, but apes and monkeys didn't, of course, live fifty million years ago. Little climbing and jumping primates called prosimians did, and they left particularly abundant fossils in the subtropical forests of North America and Eurasia. Surviving prosimians, which have changed little, live in the tropics today, but many species favor habitat outside full rain forest canopy, as though still unaccustomed to it.

I'd found at least one connection between the hammock and the brain, which also has its whisk ferns and cycads surviving under the loftier growth. Scientists speak of two older brains under the enlarged neocortex we share with apes, which is associated with speech, toolmaking, and other human traits. Directly beneath the neocortex is the limbic system, which we share with all mammals, and under that is another system, including the hypothalamus and basal ganglia, which is basically the same as reptiles' brains.

The analogy could go further. As the hammock contains not only whisk ferns and cycads, but most other kinds of plants that ever evolved — algae, mosses, club mosses, true ferns — one could say that the brain contains elements also of amphibians, fishes, invertebrates, and so on back to the individual eucaryotic cells. As the hammock's higher plants depend on the fungi, algae, lichens, mosses, and herbs that compose its soil, the brain's higher functions depend on its lower ones. Indeed, at the lowest living level, the cellular one, brain and hammock depend on the same things.

Gars and Rays

I TRIED A different approach on my next visit to the hammock. I canoed up the Halifax River to Bulow Creek, hoping it might provide an easier entrance. I imagined gliding up some quiet swamp inlet into the heart of the woods, then simply following the current back out at day's end.

I might have considered Audubon's experience, but was no longer faced with the wilderness journey that it had been for the "three white men." The Halifax is now part of the Army Corps of Engineers' inland waterway, and the lower reach of Bulow Creek has been channelized for mosquito control. It's not a bad channelization as they go, a date palm–bordered canal, but things got more interesting upstream of it.

White ibis, wood storks, and anhingas appeared along the unchannelized marshy banks, seeming wilder than the herons and egrets along the waterway. Storks and ibis had been the commonest birds when I'd canoed through the Okefenokee, the ibis croaking raucously in the morning mist, the storks soaring overhead with the vultures. The anhingas looked prehistoric, swimming with only their snakelike heads sticking out of the water. Beneath them, things were even more primeval.

Clouds of silt exploded from the bottom as big gars shot away into the murk. Some of the long-nosed, snaggletoothed fish didn't move as I approached, resting on the bottom like logs. They were probably asleep, which gars seem to be a lot of the time. Gars take life easily and haven't changed much since the first bony fishes evolved in swampy Paleozoic waters. They are so well adapted to swamps that they can stick their snouts out of the water and gulp air when droughts cut their dissolved oxygen supply. When I touched one sleeper with a paddle, however, it woke up and fled so quickly that it jolted my arm like an electric shock.

I entered an even muddier marsh channel and found an even more ancient creature. The channel was full of moving shapes, but I couldn't see them because of the mud they threw up. Then a pair of eyes became visible on the bottom as the water ahead cleared for a moment. When the canoe's shadow passed over them, a startled ray emerged from the muck and undulated away. Related to sharks, rays have cartilage skeletons that link them to the earliest fishes of all.

The water was getting shallow, the mosquitoes and marsh gas thick, so I backed out to the creek again, not wanting to get out and push like Audubon's "hands." I'd stepped on a stingray once at the beach, and it had been like having my foot slammed in a door, although the pain had gone away in a half hour or so. The rays in the marsh might have been electric rays rather than stingrays, but I didn't want to try that either.

Still, it was exhilarating to watch the ray emerge spectrally from the ooze and feel the power of the gar's muscles. It was a little like having a fish on a hook. It made me feel connected, powerful, and I began to think I was getting somewhere with my aquatic approach. Then I reached the hammock, and things got bewildering again.

The creek water had been getting more opaque as I went upstream because of swamp tannins. At least I could see the odd crab or mullet near the water's surface. But the hammock itself proved quite impenetrable. A wall of palmetto, red cedar, baccharis, smilax, prickly pear, wax myrtle, and sumac stood between me and its secrets. I could climb out on a few footwide sand beaches, but after that there was nothing to do but crawl among the sand burs and cactus spines, and I couldn't see more than a few feet into it.

It reminded me of a fishing trip on the Halifax with my parents in the 1950s. The vast (for a nine-year-old) expanse of mangrove and sea oxeye beside the river had been ex-hilarating at first, but I'd begun to get restless as the day's leisurely trolling proceeded. The procession of hammock, scrub, and salt marsh seemed unchangeable, never produc-ing the bears and panthers I craved. By afternoon, my brain had begun compensating helpfully for the disappointment. I imagined muscular feline hindquarters receding into the wax myrtle and announced this to the adults — not a promis-ing start in wildlife observation.

I evidently hadn't learned much in thirty years. The liveli-ness of rivers doesn't connect easily with that of forests, because forests tend to be impenetrable beside rivers. The abundant water and light grow green walls, which is an ob-vious ecological phenomenon, but somehow a surprising psychological one. We expect to be led into things by water, that traversable, transparent medium. Rivers are the easiest way of traveling through trackless forest. Yet one can travel hundreds of miles on a forest river and never see more than a few feet into the trees.

I couldn't even see into the saw grass marsh on the other side of the creek, because the marsh plants also stood way over my head as I sat in the canoe. I, on the other hand, was so visible and noisy as I fumbled with attempted landings, that everything with more sense than a mullet had disappeared. It was getting late, and I set off for the long, choppy paddle back across the Tomoka estuary.

Missing Links

MY EXPERIMENT seemed to be proceeding backwards. I hadn't gotten lost in my canoe simply because
I hadn't even gotten into the woods. I seemed better equipped
to make connections with fish than with forest. Humans have
lost the fear of water that makes great apes unwilling to cross
streams, but in the process we've become afraid of forests.
This might be another example of the suppression of innate
brain functions that has made us so panicky about getting lost.

It would be interesting to know just when and how humans
made the switch from water phobia to forest phobia. Of
course, many people are still afraid of water, and we still have
to be taught to swim. But I think civilization generally is hap-
pier with the wide open spaces of water than with the knots
and tangles of forest: it's easier to know where you are and
where you're going.

Perhaps the switch developed along with the sense of time.
Time tends to stand still in a forest. The trees don't move
much, and even seasonal changes don't have a destination.
Rivers are always going places, however, and as humans fanned
out from Africa they must have followed them, first in the
easily traversable valleys, then in boats. We had certain innate abilities to do so. The binocular vision inherited from

39

treetop brachiators made it possible to look across water or into it. I think water and forest have even become confused in our brains. I've sometimes dreamed of swimming through forests in water, a pleasant sensation. The water isn't too watery though: it's clear and shining, more like liquid air than murky water.

Our expanded sense of time has been highly useful, of course. It has allowed us to see all kind of things that were invisible in the forest. Yet in becoming farsighted, we seem to have lost or forgotten bits of near and peripheral vision. For example, we can now see, through paleontology, right back to the beginning of the planet and the origin and development of most of the major phyla of organisms. Yet we probably know less about the origins of the forests that evolved us, and of ourselves, than we do about those of gars and rays. There are good reasons for this, of course. Gars and rays have been around much longer than primates have and so have left many more fossils to study. Still, it's an odd position for such a self-conscious being.

We still don't know how flowering plants evolved, although paleobotanists have been saying the equivalent of "any day now" for about a century. Confusions erupt and subside. Palms, for example, are not considered primitive angiosperms. There's nothing conelike about their fruits, and their tiny flowers aren't at all like the big, floppy ones of magnolia. Yet, for a while, a fossil seemed to indicate palms were the oldest flowering plants. In 1956, a sandstone fossil of palmlike leaves and stems came to light in Colorado. It dated from the Triassic period, about a hundred million years before the magnolia fossils of the Cretaceous period, which shook up the general belief that angiosperms started in the Cretaceous.

Specialists have since decided the Colorado fossil isn't a palm, or at least that there's nothing exclusively palmlike about it. Nobody knows exactly what it is because the fossil is only an impression of the plant's leaves and stem, not the whole plant petrified. If it were whole, its anatomy would tell whether it was an angiosperm or simply a kind of fern or gymnosperm, but we can only see a cast of it, as though a cosmic prankster had put it there just to torment paleo-botanists.

The Colorado fossil wouldn't even solve the angiosperm question if it were a palm, because we still wouldn't know what *its* ancestors were. We don't even know if flowering plants have a common ancestor. Monocots, such as palms, are so different from dicots, such as magnolias, that they could very well have separate ancestries. There's an ample variety of possible ancestors — cycads, seed ferns, joint ferns, podo-carps, ginkgoes and other ambiguous gymnosperms.

If a missing link between gymnosperms and angiosperms is ever found, paleobotanists will probably be as perplexed as enlightened by it. Paleoanthropology has certainly had perplexities with its own links, one of which was a human prank rather than a cosmic one. Piltdown Man, concocted by still unidentified (but widely suspected) personages out of an orangutan's jaw and a modern man's skull, seemed to show that the first human ancestor had a man's brain in an ape's body. Genuine fossils have since shown the opposite, that early hominids such as *Australopithecus* had apelike brains in manlike bodies. But how did the manlike bodies originate?

Fossils haven't helped much there as yet. A fossil primate called *Ramapithecus* has somewhat manlike teeth, but only its teeth and a few skull fragments have been found. An earlier creature named *Propliopithecus* may have lived in a savanna environment, and thus run about on the ground instead of staying in the trees like early apes, but it too left only teeth and skull fragments. Before that, connections unravel into the mob of little prosimians to whose living descendants we give names that acknowledge their odd humanoid echoes— bushbabies, lemurs (Latin for ghost), spectral tarsiers. Saucer-eyed, long-fingered tarsiers hop through undergrowth in pursuit of insects, lead monogamous lives and have been reported creeping into camps to play with the embers of fires.

Genetically, we are enough like living African apes, chimpanzees and gorillas to suggest we diverged from a common ancestor, presumably an apelike one, no more than six or seven million years ago. There are still no fossils to prove it, and even if they are found, they still won't answer the question that agitates us the most, which is not how the human body evolved but how the human brain did. We probably know more about a gar's brain evolution than a human's.

Former Inhabitants

I WENT TO the hammock on foot the next time. It was a cool day but a still one, and the mosquitoes were worse than they'd ever been, although nighttime temperatures were dropping into the thirties. I wondered if heavy rains of a few days before had stimulated a hatch. From their banded legs, I knew they were aëdes mosquitoes, which breed in tree holes and bromeliads when rain fills them.

Spurred by the mosquitoes, I rapidly followed my memorized route back to the swamp. It hadn't changed. The mosquito fish splashed, the palmetto fronds rustled, the whisk fern sat silent. I decided to follow the gloomy streambed where I'd turned back the previous time. It offered dry footing and mosquito-inhibiting breezes.

The bed cut into higher ground as I proceeded, and it bent back and forth a lot, as streambeds will. The roots, vines, rotten logs and leaf piles along the undercut bank suggested careful placement of hands and feet, but I didn't see any snakes, not even the little brown water snakes that frequent Florida streamsides in winter, sunning on overhanging boughs so that canoeists come nose to nose with them.

As the ground got higher and drier, patches of longleaf pine savanna and sand pine scrub interrupted the hardwood canopy forest. The stout longleafs and spindly sand pines seemed less tropical than the hardwoods (although pines grow in the Caribbean and Central America) because they lacked the lush epiphytic covering of bromeliads, resurrection ferns and greenfly orchids on the hardwood branches. The hardwoods were moving in, though. The grassy spaces between the pines were dotted with live oak seedlings, planted there by jays and squirrels. Unless fire or other disturbance prevented it, the oaks would shade out any pine seedlings, and the other hardwoods — red mulberries, water hickories, red bays, Carolina ashes, sweet gums, laurel oaks, persimmons — would move in.

It looked as though magnolia would eventually become the dominant tree in the hammock. One might think more modern trees like elm or maple, with multitudes of small, winged seeds, would outbreed primitive magnolia with its clumsy fruits, but magnolia can grow in shade. Its big evergreen leaves give it a long-term advantage over deciduous trees in northern Florida's climate. Most of the seedlings in the hammock were magnolias, and they seemed likely to replace the spreading live oaks that were the biggest trees in the hammock.

The live oaks were so big that they probably were the very trees that had sprouted in Bulow Ville's abandoned fields after the Seminoles burned the place. If so, they were the only evidence that cane and indigo fields had once been there. I saw none of the relics that indicate former farmland in northern woods — no stone walls, sunken roads, or cellar holes. Except for the overgrown mill walls to the north, Bulow Ville had vanished without a trace. Of course, it hadn't lasted long to begin with, only fourteen years after its first owner, an Englishman named James Russel, had acquired it from the Spanish by "calling aloud, throwing sand, breaking branches and other things indicating possession" in front of officials.

The officials must have enjoyed this performance. Russel died promptly, perhaps from embarrassment, and a wealthy South Carolinian named Charles W. Bulow bought and developed the property, leaving it to his son when he died two years later.

John Bulow, Audubon's eventual host, was sixteen when his father died, and he went to school in Paris while trustees managed the estate. At twenty-one, he assumed control of what was then the richest plantation in Florida, with a thousand acres in cane, twelve hundred in cotton, and three or four hundred black slaves. Besides the sugar mill, finished in 1831 at the then dizzying cost of forty thousand dollars, it included enough buildings for a smallish town — manor house, forty slaves' houses, barns, corn houses, gins, and a blacksmith shop.

I wondered what young Bulow had thought about the "eternal labyrinth of waters and marshes . . . surrounded by interminable swamp" that surrounded his posh patrimony. Judging from the debacle he'd led Audubon into on the Halifax, he hadn't thought too much about it. Yet he doesn't seem to have been entirely the empty-headed young squire, since the plantation prospered and he was said to have enjoyed reading novels as well as drinking wine and "other devilment learned in Paris," as one of the founders of Ormond Beach put it. Of course, as owner of a small principality, Bulow didn't really have to think about the surrounding woods, at least, not until the Seminoles emerged from them to burn him out.

I did find evidence of human occupation that day, although it had nothing to do with Bulow Ville. The streambed meandered out of the astringent-smelling pines back into the hardwoods, which got thicker and shadier until a patch of sunlight showed through the branches. I'd come to one of the developer's bulldozings. Some animals had beaten a wavering path through the pine seedlings, dog fennel, and pokeweed growing in the abandoned track, and I thought I might reach Bulow Creek by following it eastward. I made another twig arrow to remember the streambed by, and turned onto the path.

The track was wide enough for two bulldozers, but the golden silk spiders had spun their webs across anyway. They were easier to see in full sunlight, at least, and I only walked into a few. The usual mysterious sounds came from the saw palmetto, and a little white-tailed doe made a brief appearance. I'd never encountered shyer deer than in Florida, but then I'd never seen as many hunting dogs loose in the woods as in Florida.

The ground got lower and damper after I'd walked a little while. A white patch on the ground caught my eye because, although partly brush-covered, it contrasted with the black muck soil. It was a calcified and sun-bleached pile of mollusk shells. I first thought they were just some subfossil shells turned up by the bulldozers, but they seemed too concentrated for that, and I remembered that the aboriginal Timucuan Indians had built their villages on mounds of discarded shellfish.

The Timucuans and their antecedents lived in Florida long enough to accumulate many impressive shell piles. When Europeans arrived, Indian populations were so large that the account of Hernando de Soto's expedition reads more like a trip through the English countryside than Audubon's wilderness flounderings. De Soto described one teeming village after another, although there were some primitive traits, such as the necessity of guarding mortuaries after dark so panthers wouldn't eat the dead.

Even after Florida Indians had been dying of European diseases for three centuries, the colonial American naturalist William Bartram described many impressive ruins, such as

46

a "magnificent Indian Mount" near Lake George, which is about forty miles inland from Bulow Hammock. "A noble Indian highway . . . led from the great mount, on a straight line, three quarters of a mile . . . terminated by palms and laurel magnolias, on the verge of an oblong artificial lake, which was on the edge of an extensive green level savanna. This grand highway was about fifty yards wide, sunk a little below the common level . . . neither nature nor art could anywhere present a more striking contrast, as you approached this savanna. The glittering water pond played on the sight, through the dark grove, like a diamond on the bosom of the illumined savanna."

The Bulow Hammock shell mounds might have been more imposing in Bartram's time, but now they were little more than lumps in the brush. Perhaps they'd been leveled during the clearing of Bulow Ville. I still felt an urge to poke around in them. I suppressed it, however, partly out of laziness, partly from guilty awareness that it would be vandalism to get my unschooled fingers into an unexcavated archaeological site. I walked on eastward, but the track soon ended in a wax myrtle and baccharis thicket as the ground got swampier. I glimpsed open sky through the shrubs and red cedars and pushed through them, hoping I'd finally reached the creek, which may seem paradoxical considering how hard I'd been trying to get away from the creek on my previous visit. Anyway, all I'd reached was the saw grass marsh, which pleased the mosquitoes. It was getting late. I turned back and retraced the streambed and swamp successfully, although they looked strikingly different going north than they had going south.

Near the mill ruins, I met the park ranger, a stocky moustached young man. He'd seen my car and wondered what I was doing. There were poachers around, and he was solicitous of some wild turkeys he suspected of frequenting the hammock.

"You can tell if they're around by their scratchings in the sand," he said, referring to the turkeys. "You seen any scratchings like this?" He scratched in the sand with his toe. "They sure are neat birds."

His accent and passion for wild turkeys suggested a background like that of the poachers he was worried about. He also was worried about gopher tortoises, which poachers also coveted, and he showed me the marks tortoises make in the sand. I told him I hadn't seen any turkey or tortoise marks, but that I had seen a golden silk spider eating an anole lizard.

"I've never seen *that*," he replied, a little appalled, a little incredulous, maybe a little jealous I'd seen something in his hammock that he hadn't. We were standing beside his pickup, which he'd driven a little way down a track (people with regular business in hammocks don't brave the bugs more than they have to), and I noticed several anole tails, and one anole snout, protruding from its hood. The lizards had turned a delicate pearl gray, as close as they could get, I supposed, to the blue-gray of the state park truck.

"They like to get under there for the warmth," the ranger explained. "On a cold morning, I've been walking along here and had them fall out of the trees at my feet, just stiff with cold. When I take them inside where it's warm, they jump up and run off."

I mentioned I'd been walking southeast in the direction of Bulow Creek and asked if the shell mounds were Indian sites. I could see him getting wary of me again. I probably looked more like an artifact poacher than a turkey poacher.

"Oh yeah, the species of Indian that lived here ate mostly shellfish. Uh, you haven't been digging in them, have you?"

I pled innocence, and the ranger explained that the mounds were to be excavated by a university archaeological project when it got around to them. I was a little startled, meanwhile, by what he'd said about a "species" of Indian. I felt like telling him that anthropologists now classify all people who've lived in the past fifty thousand years not only in the same species but in the same subspecies, *Homo sapiens sapiens.* I didn't, partly from laziness, partly from not wanting to seem rude.

"You've been pretty far in there if you've been to the mounds," he said. "You could get lost in there."

"I know."

The Human Organism

I WENT TO the beach the next morning. Even in cool weather, there were always people on it, walking up and down in front of the condominiums, isolated figures receding to the north and south. The morning was sunny and calm, if not warm, and some sunbathers had joined the dog-walkers, surf fishermen, motorcyclists, and surfers. A few ghost crabs had ventured out of their burrows, like pale sand clots come to life among the dog feces, tar spots, plastic bags, cigarette butts, and candy wrappers that had come to rival sargassum weed's abundance since my childhood.

Everybody on the beach was white, as usual. A good-sized black community lived in Ormond Beach, but they didn't seem to cross the Halifax much except to work in big houses. They fished from the bridges rather than the beach. It was a low-key kind of segregation but, perhaps because so inconspicuous, a little perplexing. It was so woven into the fabric of the place. The blacks didn't occupy a devastated inner city; in fact, their downtown neighborhood, shaded by big magnolias and mimosas, was more pleasant, and safer from hurricanes, than the affluent barrier island. Yet they seemed more restricted than in the North. It was one of the things that outsiders wonder about, then put out of their

heads because there doesn't seem to be any way of compre-
hending it.

I was in a perplexed frame of mind, anyway, because of
the ranger's remark of the day before. His "species of Indian"
sounded more like careless usage than racism, there being
no Indians left in the vicinity to be racist about, yet it evoked
a mental vertigo as I regarded the bare bodies around me
in the sand. These were organisms, like saw palmettoes and
whisk ferns? They'd evolved from another organism that
looked like a chimpanzee, except with shoulders, buttocks,
and calves?

Our confidence in the human organism as the measure
of all things seems to exceed any certitude about what that
organism might be. Our idea of humanity is as tangled in
evolutionary and historical confusion as the Bulow Hammock
Indian mounds are in saw palmetto and wax myrtle. The
segregation on the beach was one such confusion, based on
the nineteenth century's superficial but convenient notion
that some people might be less human than others because
they were "lower" on an evolutionary scale that was then un-
cluttered by much fossil evidence.

Nineteenth-century John James Audubon and John Muir
reflected this attitude in their remarks on blacks in Florida.
Yet its superficiality is evident from the *Travels* of William
Bartram, who visited Florida only fifty years before Audubon,
but who apparently had a quite different notion of races,
based on the Linnaean outlook rather than the Darwinian
one. While Muir and Audubon seemed to see blacks and Indians as biologically alien, with different mental and physical
capacities than whites, Bartram drew no biological distinc-
tions between the races at the same time he was identifying
numerous new plant and animal species. It wasn't that Bartram

was at ease with other races — the *Travels* is candid about his fear at meeting blacks and Indians alone in the woods — but his fear seems less alienated.

Of course, Bartram spent much more time with blacks and Indians than Muir or Audubon did. Not only did he make lengthy visits to Seminole towns during the explorations in the 1770s that resulted in his book, but he spent a year living alone with six black slaves in a swamp near Picolata on the St. Johns River in 1766. It must have been quite an experience. He'd been visiting Florida with his naturalist father, John, in 1765 and had become so taken with the place (or so deranged by an unhappy love affair) that he'd decided to stay and start a plantation after his father left. John had grumbled at this "frolick," but, a free-thinking Philadelphia Quaker, he had furnished William with the slaves and other plantation-starting supplies before leaving.

It had been a disastrous decision. Picolata, about fifty miles northwest of Bulow Hammock, was "the least agreeable of all the places I have seen," according to a friend of John's, Henry Lauren. Only two of the slaves had been capable of working, and one of these had been "so insolent as to threaten" his proprietor's life. The proprietor had lived in "a hovel, extremely confined . . . not proof against the weather," his provisions "scanty, even to penury." He'd had fever on Lauren's first visit, and "looked very poorly" on the second.

If any situation was calculated to turn a man into a racist, or a maniac, Bartram's plantation career would seem to have been it. Yet he didn't become either. It's one of the mysteries of American history. I wondered how *he* had slept at night: he hadn't had to close his eyes to see bony faces. The mystery will probably never be solved, because Bartram evidently never wrote anything on the experience. Perhaps having to live in the same squalor as the slaves kept him from going off the deep end by minimizing the alienation that feeds racism and madness.

Twentieth-century ideas support the eighteenth-century perception of the human organism over the nineteen-century one. Genetic studies show more variation *within* races than among them, and fossils demonstrate no evolutionary step-ladder from tropical, black humans to temperate, white ones. Of course, hominids did evolve first in tropical Africa, yet the temperate regions of Asia and Europe were pioneered not by *Homo sapiens* but by *Homo erectus,* the big-jawed ancestral species whose brain-eating habits near Peking thrilled me in fourth grade. *Homo sapiens* didn't appear until *H. erectus* had been inhabiting the subtropical and temperate zones for a million years and, although there is evidence that *H. sapiens* evolved first in Africa, there is no evidence that we have evolved significantly since then. The small jaws and brows, protruding chins, light bones, and large brains that characterize us are basically the same in the early African fossils as in later European ones.

According to present ideas, *Homo sapiens* is unlikely to change much biologically because we have become so wide-spread and numerous. Populations must be isolated for genetic mutation to change them significantly from other populations, and no modern human population is isolated. Anthropologists expect future human evolution to be cultural rather than biological, and although cultural change can significantly affect behavior, there is not yet evidence that it can change the organism much. Genes keep replicating legs and arms capable of killing elephants in bodies required only to climb in and out of automobiles. They keep reproducing the same size brains in nuclear physicists as they did in elephant hunters.

Modern evolutionary ideas can seem to confirm a faith in the organism's supremacy. Genetically uniform, evolutionarily stabilized, the human body can seem a powerful platform from which to conquer the universe, a kind of evolutionary launching pad. Yet the very imperviousness to vast cultural change that makes the organism seem supreme can raise some odd questions about its role.

According to neo-Darwinian theory, new species such as *H. sapiens* succeed because of fitness, because new traits let them adapt to environment in new ways. A recent corollary, punctuated equilibrium, suggests that new species can emerge rapidly when environmental changes create new conditions. *Homo sapiens* may have been better fitted than *H. erectus* for a drying African climate by a capacity for greater social organization and more elaborate technology. A considerably enlarged brain would have been the major factor in this increased capacity.

But why should the same brain that fitted us for elephant hunting in a drying Africa now fit us equally well, apparently, for so many other things? Perhaps it is simply because a bigger brain provides increased ability to adapt to new environments. If the organism is supreme and the brain is a built-in survival computer, this is self-evident. But do organs always serve the organism so efficiently? They aren't really machines, but groups of cells, and these have a certain evolutionary potential of their own.

Various cell types, including the nerve cells that comprise the brain, have maintained characteristic traits so long throughout the planet's evolution that some scientists suspect them of having had quite different, free-living ancestors. When minced living tissues are placed in a nutrient bath, the scattered nerve cells migrate to reunite with other nerve cells, skin cells with skin cells, and so on. Of course, organisms have immune systems to keep their own nerve cells segregated from others', yet from a cellular viewpoint, at least, life's evolution might be less a matter of radiation into organisms than one of a planetary mat of cells in which the basic cell types are more significant than the evanescent bodies they occupy. Where the organism sees bodies standing or striding about purposefully, the cell would see a vast, shifting edifice or grid in which groups of one cell type, such as brain cells, might signify more than groups of organs, or might evolve at different rates.

We are familiar with one form of independent evolutionary potential, when cells evolve backwards toward the anaerobic disorganization of carcinoma. What if cells can grow in an organized way that is sometimes somehow independent of the entire organism's fitness, becoming a kind of evolutionary tumor? This is a bizarre idea, but who will deny that the organ that conceived and contrived the thermonuclear explosion is bizarre? At least the notion makes a stab at explaining the phenomenon that has produced not only technology and society far beyond a fitness for Pleistocene Africa, but insanity, mass delusions, the "peaceful" atom, art, homosexuality, and baseball.

There may be other evolutionary tumors besides the brain. Its evolution may have more in common with the evolution of flowers than paleontological obscurity. We can't necessarily assume, as we generally do, that flowers evolved to make plants more fit through reproductive efficiency. Such efficiency could be more a result of flowering plant evolution than a cause. Primitive survivors such as magnolias suggest that early flowering plants were rather clumsy reproducers, their large blossoms producing a few heavy seeds that simply crashed to the ground and lay there, prey to any passing animal. Gymnosperms such as *Sequoia* were blanketing the ground with thousands of small, winged seeds at that time. Flowers could have evolved not because they produced more and better seed, but from some evolutionary cause in the reproductive tissues themselves.

Brains and flowers might even have had the same evolutionary cause: they might be cases of arrested development. The human brain gets larger than the ape's because human infants take much longer to mature, and the brain keeps growing. This prolonged maturation is thought to have been a response to environmental stress, perhaps the drying African climate. The first flowers may also have appeared on plants whose reproductive maturation was slowed by stress. The structure of magnolia flowers suggests that petals developed from the overgrown cone scales of some ancient gymnosperm. The same *kind* of stress might even have caused brain and flower evolution. Like the Pleistocene era that produced *Homo sapiens,* the Cretaceous epoch included episodes of drying climate.

Of course, brains and flowers are very different things, as are hominids and angiosperms. Flowers grow on every angiosperm, but a greatly enlarged brain grows on only one living hominid—indeed, only on one living primate: *Homo sapiens.* Still, humans aren't the only mammals with big brains. The large brains of whales and dolphins are unlikely to have resulted from the stress of drying climate, but we can be even less sure that a large brain is required for catching fish than it is for hunting elephants. Perhaps the large mammal brain is at a stage comparable to that of the early angiosperms, when only a few plants bore flowers.

Yet if large brains didn't evolve simply to promote fitness and serve as survival computers, what are they doing here? Flower evolution comes to mind. If flowers evolved somewhat independently of the needs of the plants they grew on, they didn't evolve in a vacuum. They evolved, to some degree, in *independent* relationship with surrounding ecosystems. Flowers developed complex ecological relationships with insects and other pollinating organisms that have little to do with the whole plant. Bees don't visit red bay flowers because they're interested in red bay trees. The tree's reproductive benefit is a side effect of the bee-flower relationship.

The brain might have its own bees, in some sense. As a cell colony with a vast capacity for information storage, it might store much information of only marginal significance to the whole organism. Just as a flower stores information about the tastes, habits, and even shapes of pollinating insects in order to mimic them and thus attract the insects, the brain might have mimetic agendas in which the entire organism is peripheral. The brain is a much bigger and more complex organ than the flower. Spread out, its convolutions assume the dimensions of a hearth rug. What information would two million years of human evolution have stored, on top of the hundreds of millions of years of evolution built into its older structures?

The Stinkpots

THE HAMMOCK gave me a kind of seminar in the unexpected the next time I went in. The weather had suddenly turned steamy hot. Such abrupt changes were among the things that drove Audubon crazy about Florida. "The climate here is the most changeable I ever saw," he complained, "down to forty-five and then a smart frost after which the southerly winds have made us all sweat at our drawings."

Mosquitoes and ticks seemed rather invigorated after the cold snap, but not all animals were unscathed. Many golden silk spiders were dead in their webs, although still so colorful that only a shriveled aspect to their abdomens evinced their demise. A rotund little white spider sat on one corpse, perhaps lying in wait for carrion insects. The green and pink spiders I'd seen on the first walk had disappeared.

Dead and disappearing spiders seemed appropriate for a time when most of the trees were shedding their leaves, even if the maples were also budding out, and the magnolias and live oaks were *not* shedding their leaves. When I made my way to the palmetto swamp, however, I stumbled upon a creature that seemed to have almost nothing appropriate about it. Apparently unfazed by the frost, the biggest stick insect I'd ever seen strode across the leaf litter. Stick insects are mainly tropical animals, and the few species that live in the northern United States disappear promptly with the cold weather. They also stay in the trees and bushes, where their resemblance to sticks makes them hard to see. This Florida stick insect, which was light brown with black stripes, seemed to defy its category.

I picked it up, and it sprayed my hand with a pungent, turpentine-smelling substance that slightly irritated my eyes and nose even at arm's length. It wasn't as defenseless as it seemed, although this didn't explain why, looking like a stick, it chose to amble over the ground when there were trees to climb everywhere. I put it down, and it ambled away. (I later encountered others of this species on the ground.)

A marsh breeze coursed through the swamp, bending some palmettoes almost horizontally. Dead fronds crashed unnervingly to the ground, but there was something exhilarating about the tossing of branches, backlit by the westering sun. Red and yellow hardwood leaves fluttered to the ground in flocks, like goldfinches and cardinals. The air felt cooler and drier after the breeze died, as though a new weather front was moving in. The mosquitoes seemed less insistent.

I followed the dry streambed south again, continuing past the track to the shell mounds. The bed quickly got narrower and shallower; it was a very young stream, perhaps started from an erosion gully in the Bulow Ville fields. The trees in this part of the hammock were young too and close-growing. They admitted little sunlight, and the farther I went, the gloomier it seemed. I thought of the lizard in the spider web again.

It was getting late, but I kept on. I had a feeling I'd get somewhere. I crossed another bulldozed track, passed through more second growth, and got somewhere, to a large drainage ditch. Cut deep and straight into the white sand, it evidently drained pasture land to the west of the hammock. It was much too new to have been part of Bulow Ville, although there were some good-size saplings on its spoil banks.

There was a whistling sound, and a resplendent wood duck drake flew up the ditch, then veered into the trees when he saw me. I climbed out of the streambed, trying to get a better look at him and found myself at the edge of a little sinkhole. Holes caused by groundwater undermining limestone bedrock are common in Florida hammocks and contribute to their air of intricate concealment. Some are huge, full of azure water boiling up from springs. This one was little more than a puddle in a pit, a stew of brown leaves obscuring its bottom.

It was full of mosquito fish anyway, and they made their usual agitations as I approached. Something else was moving in the water, something black and shiny. It didn't look like anything I'd ever seen before. It seemed to have a hard shell, and I wondered if I'd stumbled on some kind of giant, freshwater crab. I'd never heard of such a thing in Florida. Then I looked closer and saw that it was a small turtle.

It pulled its head underwater as I loomed above, but remained in sight. It wasn't one of the cooter turtles commonly seen basking along Florida waterways. It was shaped like a small snapping turtle, and I thought it might be a young snapper until my eyes got better at distinguishing reptile carapace from fallen leaves. Then I knew this was no immature snapper, because there was another turtle behind the first, and they were copulating. There was no doubt about that. The first turtle, evidently the female, couldn't move without dragging the second along behind her.

We blinked at each other a moment, then the female took

alarm and began to burrow into the fallen leaves. She accomplished this quickly, but it left her mate in an awkward position. As she burrowed, he gradually was upended, still coupled to her, until he lay on his back, legs waving. I'd seldom seen a healthy animal in its native habitat look so helpless. As the female continued burrowing, she slowly drew him under the leaves, still upended, still gesticulating feebly. His face was the last to disappear, and it looked distinctly sheepish.

I didn't know whether to laugh or cry. It was ridiculous, but it was a little horrible: to be pulled helplessly into the ooze while pursuing the supreme pleasure of life. It was like a jungle-movie nightmare: reptiles copulating in slime, life an illusory exhalation from ooze. I went away with a creeping sensation.

Yet I felt a peculiar happiness walking back. The hammock had changed. The setting sun's light slipped under the tree canopy and reflected a deep maroon from the fallen maple and sweet gum leaves. It was somehow intoxicating, as though the air was hazy not with terpenes and water vapor but with a good Beaujolais.

I certainly had found *something*. Turtles are seldom seen mating, even more seldom in December. The turtles in the sinkhole were musk turtles (also called stinkpots because of the smell of their musk), among the most prolific of turtles, but even they are supposed to mate in spring, even in Florida. This defiance of expectation was impressive, as though the turtles might know something we don't.

The maroon light changed to topaz as I got back into the older woods, where yellow-leaved hickories, ashes, and hornbeams predominated over maples. Something was crashing about in the underbrush, and I looked that way, expecting to see a squirrel. It sounded like some such nimble animal bounding over the leaf litter. Another surprise: it was an armadillo, bounding nimbly through the leaf litter. I'd assumed that a shelled mammal would be as sedate as a turtle. Burdened by no such assumption, the armadillo bounded away.

Problems

I'D REACHED the hammock's center at the drainage ditch — its spatial center, at least. A sand road across the ditch led south to the state highway. I didn't feel I'd arrived much of anywhere, except at confusion — tree insects on the ground, turtles mating in winter, bounding armadillos. There's nothing like a walk in the woods to fray biological generalizations. Nature can seem essentially confused, random, our notions of habits, cycles, and seasons mere comforting fictions to cloak a chaos in which a creature evolved to mimic a twig can arbitrarily abandon the trees. This can make larger questions, such as the supremacy of the organism, seem not only speculative but irrelevant.

Of course, I wouldn't have found such unruliness in New England woods in December. The turtles would have been sleeping primly in mud, the stick insects properly dead. Nature can seem more random the farther south one goes from the rigors of temperate seasons, a phenomenon humans should consider in regard to our own southern origins. Our distant ancestors accomplished some unruliness of their own. Like the stick insects, for example, they were adapted to trees but took to the ground.

Since there's no clear fossil link between early apes and hominids, we don't know how and why our early ancestors came down from the trees. A drying climate some ten million years ago may have had something to do with it by driving apes out of dwindling forests into spreading grasslands. Fossils of tree-dwelling apes are common before that time, while fossils of ground-dwelling ones are common after it. Yet tree apes couldn't simply have climbed down and walked away as droughts shrank forests. They'd need to have evolved some ground-dwelling capacity first.

It's been suggested that apes moved to the forest floor because they were getting too large to live in the trees, or because monkeys (which actually evolved *after* apes) had become more efficient in the treetops and forced them out. Fossils do show that early apes were smaller than later ones. But did apes come down from the trees because they'd gotten bigger, or did they get bigger because they'd come down? Early hominids weren't much taller than gibbons, the most arboreal living apes, although they were heavier. Did the apes have to get bigger to compete with monkeys, then have to get smaller so they could dodge lions in the savanna? Human evolution seems so tortuous one wonders how the poor things managed it.

Of course, they didn't manage it. They weren't trying to become us, which is so obvious that we generally ignore it. We think of human evolution as problem-solving, a kind of wilderness primate lab with sticks and stones instead of bananas and letter blocks. We are so deeply confident that life is a problem, and survival its reward, that it's hard to remember that this is an idea instead of a fact. Not content with seeing life as the individual organism's problem, or the species' collective one, scientific reductionists have imposed the stern duties and high rewards of problem-solving on the smallest known unit of biotic organization. The selfish gene, sociobiologists tell us, really controls the organisms and species whose DNA it inhabits in order to survive and reproduce through intricately computed breeding strategies.

The awesome fecundity of many organisms seems to support the view that survival is the problem. All organisms aren't awesomely fecund, however. And if survival is the imperative, why is there so much failure to survive? Why aren't all organisms limpetlike things, eternally clinging to the safest rocks? One can say that death is a solution to the problem of environmental change and physical wear, but it's not a solution that problem-solving civilization really much admires.

The greatest question of all, of course, is why the organism we regard as the problem-solver par excellence seems lately to be creating more deadly problems than it solves. If the enlarged human brain is an evolutionary tumor, it is beginning to seem like a malignant one. Loaded with maps, compasses, quadrants, roads and other solutions to the problem of its place on earth, it lapses into panic, withdraws into outright craziness; and there are few subjects about which we know less than the evolution of insanity.

Survival is a major evolutionary theme: we're still here after about three and a half billion years. But there is also that other great theme, extinction, and another that we call, for lack of a better word, change. We think of change as a part of problem-solving—life getting better adapted, more successful—but the evolution of flowers and brains has been considerably more than adaptation. It has created new worlds, and problems.

It's hard to see how the "problem" of human life could be solved, in an evolutionary sense. It's hard to see what it is.

If our dreams of flying have anything to do with brachiation, a lot of us still isn't down from the trees. There are odd parallels between treetop life and grassland life. One sees far, there are bright flowers and fruits near at hand. Brachiating and running seem like mirror activities, with hominid legs taking on the swinging motions of ape arms. We spend most of our lives climbing around in wooden boxes, as though our real aspiration is to reascend into the treetops.

The Savanna

THE HAMMOCK was beginning to seem too much for me. When it wasn't being secretive, it became unintelligible. The more time I spent in it, the more the sense of watchfulness I'd first perceived in it seemed to fade into indifference, as though my novelty had worn off, and it was turning a barky back on me. Or, to be less anthropomorphic, it was as though my brain had responded to some initial stimulation, then relapsed into unconsciousness. I felt that I'd read the first two pages of a book and found the rest either blank or unintelligible.

I had an urge for more open places. I'd go up the coast road to the little prairies behind the last undeveloped dunes between Ormond Beach and Flagler Beach, or to the salt marshes west of the barrier island. There were flowers, lantanas and gerardias and beach marigolds, and swarms of white butterflies. But I couldn't really get away from the sense of constriction I felt in the hammock because the open, grassy patches gave way quickly to mud or tangles of stunted bumelia and sea amyris. I sympathized with Audubon's and Muir's frustrations.

One day, I drove halfway across the state to get to an open

space big enough to stretch out in, a state preserve called Payne's Prairie near Gainesville. William Bartram knew it as the Alachua Savanna when he visited a nearby Seminole town in 1775, coming out of the surrounding hammocks into "a level green plain, above fifteen miles over, fifty miles in circumference, and scarcely any tree or bush of any kind to be seen in it." He was impressed, a little disturbed. "How the mind is agitated and bewildered at being thus, as it were, placed on the borders of a new world . . . the most sudden transition from darkness to light that can possibly be exhibited in a natural landscape."

The savanna is treeless because it is a giant sinkhole into which local streams empty, making it a marsh or even a lake during wet seasons. Bartram was surprised to have his horse sink to its belly in the water of apparent grassy meadows as he rode across. The unexpectedness of sinkholes fascinated him, particularly the flow of subterranean water that caused fish to disappear into sunken caves "where probably, they are separated from each other, by innumerable paths or secret rocky avenues; and after encountering various obstacles, and beholding new and unthought-of scenes of pleasure and disgust, after many days absence from the surface of the world emerge again from the dreary vaults and appear exulting in gladness and sporting in the transparent waters of some distant lake." Such descriptions so stirred young European romantics after the *Travels'* publication in 1792 that they stole them for novels and poems. The most famous of these was Coleridge's "Kubla Khan" with its sacred river running "through caverns measureless to man / down to a sunless sea."

I didn't find what Bartram had found at the savanna, however. I arrived in the dry season of a drought year in a series of drought years. The savanna was a brown expanse of dead broomsedge and maiden cane under a smoky sky. I couldn't walk across it because that would have disturbed a flock of sandhill cranes feeding in the middle. I climbed a pile of dead trees (the state had been pulling fencerows to return the savanna to natural conditions) and looked across.

I could barely see the other side. The gray dots of the cranes in the center resolved, when I focused my binoculars on them, into hunched, elderly looking shapes milling around like retirees at a garden party. Their cackling was surprisingly loud for such distant objects. The only other sound was occasional freeway noise from the other end of the prairie (an interstate was part of the political price of establishing a preserve). An occasional marsh hawk soared over; sparrows and towhees hopped in the weeds. A black snake crawled sluggishly up a log, then crawled down again.

The savanna was famous for snakes. Bartram seemed to find a snake under every bush there, unusual species such as coachwhips and glass snakes, snakes "entwined together" so contentedly that they didn't try to strike or escape when he "endeavored to irritate them." In the 1930s, biologist Archie Carr still found snakes everywhere in the savanna, but they became much less common after that. Carr suspected the freeway of decimating them. Blacktop roads are like heroin to snakes; the warmth attracts them at night.

Bartram saw many unusual things beside snakes in the savanna's vicinity. There were tropical elements in Florida then that have since vanished, not only Carolina parakeets, but royal palms and king vultures, the big, colorful vultures of the Amazon and Central America. There were packs of red wolves, big flocks of wild turkeys.

I began to feel depressed at the savanna's present vacancy.

71

This was reasonable, but I also began to feel panicky, which wasn't, particularly. I wasn't lost in the woods. I might have been at the beach, although beaches can be disturbing. I'd been walking on the undeveloped beach north of Ormond one day and seen a motionless spot in the distance. It had been so dark against the white sand that I was almost on top of it before I saw that it was a loggerhead turtle, crouched at the high tide line as though come ashore to lay eggs. It wouldn't be laying any more eggs, though: flies buzzed around its half-open eyes. The shrimp boats offshore probably had drowned it in their nets the night before.

But there weren't any turtles about the dessicated savanna, dead or alive. I stretched out on the log and dozed awhile. The smoke-obscured sun was getting low when I awoke, but I stayed because I wanted to see if the cranes would behave as Bartram had described. "The sonorous savanna cranes, in well-disciplined squadrons, now rising from the earth, mounted aloft in spiral circles, far above the dense atmosphere of the humid plain; they again viewed the glorious sun, and the light of day still gleaming on their polished feathers, they sung their evening hymn, then in a straight line majestically descended, and alighted in the towering Palms or lofty Pines, their secure and peaceful lodging places."

When I'd canoed across the Okefenokee Swamp, the cranes had seemed like the spirit of the wilderness. We hadn't seen them until deep in the swamp, in places where barred owls and red-shouldered hawks showed no fear of humans. Yet the cranes had honked and thrown themselves into the air the second they'd seen us coming, as though even the Okefenokee might not be lonely enough for them.

The Payne's Prairie cranes seemed more interested in grasshoppers than flight. They cackled and milled through the

sunset, perhaps saving their hymn singing for better conditions. It wasn't much of a sunset, a rusty smudge on the horizon. When it was dark, I groped my way back to the car and
drove coastward past the neon strips of Ocala, at that time
the fastest-growing town in the United States.

The Alligators

MY UNEASY vacillation between the hammock and the savanna was typical of the species. American pioneers pushed uneasily through eastern forests, cutting trees, then pushed uneasily across midwestern prairies, planting them. Humans generally have lurked around the edges of the great forests and grasslands, and for all our present dominance, we remain edgy creatures, shifting restlessly between open and closed, light and dark.

I wondered if I was simply presumptious to seek some kind of mental integration with a forest, to not be satisfied with the edge that culture has provided over nature. Segregation is advantage for the segregator. I didn't seem to be getting anywhere. There'd been nothing at the end of the green tunnel, so far, except a couple of copulating stinkpots in a puddle. Not exactly the fountain of youth. Still, there had been that unexpected vinous glow under the maples. The oldest things of earth, like turtles, are in a sense the youngest. The air is freshest over oceans and wetlands, and there's nothing older than those.

I wanted at least to reach Bulow Creek from the hammock and thought I could if I followed the drainage ditch east. I went on the morning of the day before Christmas Eve. The woods looked different with the light from the east, more summery. The warm weather had held, and some of the golden silk spiders still lived. There were flocks of yellow butterflies, and even a few zebra-striped heliconians, tropical butterflies that feed on passion vine.

I knew the way pretty well, and things had gotten a little vague with familiarity: towhees scratching in cane thickets, redbellied woodpeckers, liverworts on palmetto stumps, Span-ish moss on oak branches. It was near noon when I reached the ditch. I looked in the sinkhole, but the turtles were no-where in sight. I crossed the ditch on a log and followed it east. Soon the sky began sparkling in front of me, as it does over wetlands and water. I topped a little rise and glimpsed an expanse of saw grass and distant palmetto tops through the brush bordering the ditch. I'd reached Bulow Creek.

A movement caught my eye as I came in sight of the water. I glimpsed a scaly tail disappearing into the far side of the creek, where a path was beaten into the marsh. This was no turtle or armadillo tail; this was a tail of weight and substance, though it slipped underwater with less commotion than the stinkpots had made. There's nothing more discreet than an alligator's submergence. When I reached the bank, there was no sign of the tail's owner.

A large baccharis bush screened the creek downstream. I peered through it and saw two more alligators lying on a dark gray mudbank on the inside of a bend. Soon a third, probably the one that had just submerged, climbed briskly aboard. Its legs looked incongruously spindly as they trundled the loglike body up the bank. It flopped down companionably with the others, very much as a sunbather collapses on a beach towel.

The three alligators lay at right angles to me with their heads up, apparently aware of my presence. They were as gray as the mud, but there was no question of mistaking them for driftwood, not with their black marble eyes open. Yet they didn't look any more dangerous than sunbathers do when eyeing some suspicious-looking beach idler. Their crocodilian grins made them seem rather amiable. The largest had a blunt, upturned snout like Pogo Possum's friend Albert's.

I'd seen wild alligators before, behaving in various ways from menacing to foolish. (A young one in the Okefenokee had "escaped" by sticking its head underwater and floating motionless, rump in the air, even when I touched it with a paddle.) I'd never seen them so relaxed. We get used to seeing large, threatened animals either from a distance or in flight, not lying about the landscape as though it was their living room. Of course, it is their living room, but they've learned to vacate so promptly at our appearance that we tend to forget this.

The alligators' confiding presence pulled the landscape together in a new way, focused it. Things seemed more vivid. A passing flight of wood ibis made a post-impressionist harmony of laundry white plumage against absinthe green saw grass. A cardinal hopping in the wax myrtle sounded like something bigger, a feathered dinosaur. Sulfurous exhalations from the mud alternated with extraordinarily fresh, sweet breezes that blew up the creek like intimations of Bartram's fragrant, unviolated Florida. "A fascinating atmosphere surrounds this blissful garden; the balmy Lantana, ambrosial Citra, perfumed Crinum, perspiring their mingled odors, wafted through Zanthoxylon groves." Because I couldn't see any balmy lantanas or perfumed crinums, it was a little eerie, as though I was smelling ghost flowers, dead since the American Revolution, or at least since the previous spring. Audubon had found huge lilies blooming in the Bulow marshes in December, but I didn't.

I sat beside the creek several hours, happy just to see, hear, and smell, to feel the sun on my face. My simian, imitative side was showing. If the alligators were content just to lie there, so was I. It wasn't lonely or boring with them there. I didn't feel threatened by their presence — on the contrary. Our ancestors evolved in landscapes teeming with other kinds of animals. It would have been the empty landscape that un-nerved them, a presage of stalking predators, storm, drought, eruption.

Of course, my sense of security depended to some degree on having the alligators on the other side of the creek. William Bartram passed moments of exquisite insecurity with alligators, beating off eighteen-footers with a club, but that was before alligators learned to avoid humans, and it was in May, during the pugnacious alligator breeding season. I had less to fear sunbathing with alligators on Bulow Creek than on Ormond Beach where people have been run over by cars.

Tree shadows inched over the mudbank as the sun declined, but they didn't discourage the alligators. They sedately changed position now and then, although not to stay in the sunlight, but following inscrutable alligator whims instead. The sha-dows chilled me, however, and I restlessly climbed a steep shell mound or spoil bank between ditch and mudbank. The top was overgrown with trees and shrubs, but my sudden ap-pearance on it startled the alligators. They took to the water with a speed that startled me.

It had been typical simian behavior: trying to get on top of things. The landscape dimmed for a while. Then a blunt gray snout appeared in the water by the mudbank and hov-ered cautiously. A moment later, the two smaller alligators hauled out briskly, and the big one followed, but a little un-easily. It lay down close to the water, looking around and shifting position frequently. The alligators obviously were as intent on getting their day of sunbathing as any bikinied vacationer in Daytona, and they weren't going to let loitering strangers spoil it. I could see why they would be, before retiring for another clammy night in their marsh burrows.

A sense of integration returned to the landscape with the alligators. The height of the mound actually enhanced it. There was a new pictorial dimension, an aerial perspective, with foreground, middle ground, background. I felt a satisfying sense of proportion: the red and gold embroidery of smilax and sumac around me; the deeper colors of creek, mudbank and alligators below me; the azure and absinthe of sky and marsh before me, divided by black palmettoes at the horizon. Kingfishers, egrets, and ibis flew past toward their evening feeding. It was a museum diorama come back to life, a brief fulfillment of the longing, wistfully expressed in cubicles of stuffed hide, plastic plants, and painted plaster, for a world not emptied by the human shadow.

Qualities

I BEGAN TO feel that I'd actually gotten somewhere in the hammock. It was a little like taking off an eye patch I hadn't known I was wearing. Things suddenly seemed more three-dimensional, solid, palpable. If anything is at the center of subtropical swamps, it is the alligator. It has not only been living in them since before the dinosaurs, it *makes* them. When alligators were almost extirpated from the Everglades in the 1960s, bird and fish populations declined because they depend on holes alligators dig in the saw grass during the dry season. The only open water in the swamp then is in the alligator holes. Alligator fossils have been found wherever the great subtropical swamp forest of which Bulow Hammock is a remnant grew — California, Kansas, Germany, China. Another alligator species still survives precariously in the Yangtze Valley.

It wasn't as though I'd never seen an alligator before. Or perhaps it was. I'd seen dozens of alligators in the Okefenokee, but they hadn't seemed as real as the ones in the hammock. Crossing the Okefenokee had been a matchless experience, but the perfection had entailed a certain detachment. I might have been visiting another world, which had been part of the attraction, and of course I'd expected alligators in the Okefenokee. I hadn't expected them in the hammock, and because it was a place I'd known most of my life, finding them there had been a little like finding them in myself, like stumbling on a lazy, insouciant vitality at the center of my own mind.

We're used to thinking of the reptile mind as nasty, violent, and dull. There's even been a fashion of blaming wars on an atavistic reptilian will to power. Yet reptiles are no more aggressive than birds or mammals, and probably less violent, because less fearful. No wild bird or mammal allows itself to be picked up and handled as many snake species will. There's a kind of tranquillity in their simplicity. Human fear of reptiles is not simple and reptilian, but convoluted and mammalian.

Since the human brain's major growth has not been in its old, reptilian part, it is unfair to blame our destructiveness on it. The reptile part of our brains would give us rather inoffensive, calm lives if uninterfered with by the neocortex. Anybody who thinks that an enlarged neocortex is a recipe for peace and quiet is ignoring the evolutionary evidence, which shows a billion years of relative stability before the enlarged neocortex and a million years of rapidly increasing hysteria after it.

One of the things that had made my unexpected panic in the western mountains so disturbing had been a suspicion that it came from the center of my brain, from a realm of basic organic turmoil and chaos down there. I'd been afraid I was a nova of sensibility and reason ever-ready to implode into a black hole. Yet the timid, confiding alligators seemed to contradict this. It was reassuring to think that the part of my brain they represented might be older than my fears, that a scaly part of me could rest on a mudbank while the primate screamed in the trees.

I had to leave Florida then. The experiment seemed at least slightly successful. I felt I'd formed some kind of mental link with the place, and my brain apparently agreed. It stopped ambushing me in the mountains. The sudden attacks of vertigo dwindled away over the next few years. There seemed to be some kind of balancing going on. I didn't really know if it had to do with finding some alligators in a swamp, but it seemed as good a reason as any, and the alligators hadn't charged me fifty dollars an hour for the consultation.

Yet experiments have to be repeatable to be successful. How could I be sure the qualities I'd perceived in the hammock were essential to it? Qualities are notoriously hard to predict. If I'd measured the quantities of nutrients the swamp produced, I could have been fairly confident it would be similar in a couple of years. I was less sure about the qualities of tranquillity and beauty. I'd had a furtive tendency to shy away from places I'd found beautiful for fear the quality wouldn't repeat.

I hadn't really gotten far toward understanding my mind in relation to trees, particularly if the reptile part of it wasn't the source of the disturbance. It was the panicky primate part that had evolved in the trees. It was the neocortex that turned the hammock into a roller coaster ride of cowering at thickets and exulting in glades. I needed to climb farther into my neural canopy.

I went back to the hammock a few years later. I gave myself an edge this time. I went back in April. If the hammock had been beautiful in the dying season, it seemed likely to be even more so in the flowering one. But I found that I didn't understand the hammock.

The Empty Window

WHEN I DROVE down the sand road again on a still, already hot morning, the green tunnel looked exactly as it had in November two years before. Blue spiderworts and yellow cannas were blooming in the grass along the state highway, but I didn't see any spring wildflowers along the sand road. Even the new leaves of the deciduous trees didn't make the hammock look any greener.

I did find one change when I parked: a hiking trail had been cut southward to the ditch. After all the trouble I'd had groping my way into the hammock, anyone could now do it easily. It seemed to negate what I'd learned, so I turned up my nose at the newly painted white and baby blue blazes and started into the trees following my old route.

I discerned a few signs of spring as I walked. Red-eyed vireos and other migratory birds were singing, and mosquitoes were thicker than ever. If I stopped moving long enough for the local population to zero in, I found myself in mosquito world, hearing, seeing, and feeling nothing but mosquitoes. I kept walking pretty fast, maybe too fast, because I found that my old route didn't seem to work anymore. I made the turns that had led me to the palmetto swamp two years before, but they didn't now. Instead, my mosquitoes and I found ourselves in a face-high tangle of saw palmetto where large numbers of ticks joined us. (I would pick thirty ticks from skin and clothing that night.) I retraced my steps and tried the old route again, and again, until I somehow stumbled into the remembered swamp.

It looked the same, except that there was a little more water in it. The palmetto trunk on which I'd crossed the water before had rotted sufficiently to collapse under my weight this time. I lurched to the other bank, shoes only moderately muddied, and paused. A faint breeze was inconveniencing the mosquitoes. I noticed a few patches of white lizard's tail and yellow ragwort growing on the swamp floor, sunnier than under the oaks and magnolias. It wasn't much compared to the masses of flowers I'd have expected in a spring woodland.

I looked for the ancient little whisk fern I'd found on the palmetto trunk. It was there, but it was shriveled and brown, not the healthy green plant of two years before. I wondered if exceptionally cold weather that had struck Florida the winter before had killed it, but there were still a few green stems hidden among the brown ones. Perhaps it was simply an old plant, although I didn't see any young wisk ferns around, or any old ones either. If it was dying, it seemed to be the last of its race in the hammock.

Even the golden silk spiders seemed to be gone. I didn't walk into one of their webs. I wouldn't have minded their absence except that the superabundant mosquitoes were worse than spiderwebs.

I followed the streambed east toward the ditch. The bed had been almost dry before; now it was full of brown water and mosquito fish. The fallen red maple leaves that had given it a maroon glow in autumn were brown mold, and the new foliage overhead made the bed shadier and gloomier than ever. The songbirds stopped singing as the sun mounted toward noon, and the woods became silent, without even the odd rustles that had unnerved me before.

I crossed the abandoned subdivision track. The longleaf pine seedlings in it were over my head now, but the deer path was still distinct. When I reached the ditch, I looked into the stinkpots' sinkhole, but nothing moved except the inevitable mosquito fish. The puddle seemed drier, and there was a slightly putrid smell.

The fallen log that had bridged the ditch had disappeared, so I pushed toward Bulow Creek through the saw palmetto on the ditch's north bank. I made a lot of noise—Audubon had known what he was talking about when he complained of "scrambling through the vilest thickets"—and no alligators were in sight when I finally reached the water. I could bare-ly see the mudbank where they'd lain two years before. Heavy brush screened the ditch.

It was like trying to watch a street from a barred and recessed cellar window, although I didn't seem to be missing much. I crouched there a long time, but glimpsed not an ibis or anhinga, nor even a heron. The place looked vacated, as though the wildlife had moved away en masse. What had seemed a diorama come to life now seemed a diorama gone to seed, the specimens lost, even the background faded and marred.

Giant Eggs

I REALIZED the mistake I'd made. I'd come to the hammock with temperate preconceptions. Spring is a period of growth and reproduction in temperate deciduous woods because water and sunlight are at a peak on the forest floor. In summer, the tree canopy uses most of the available water and sunlight, so wildflowers and other small ground organisms reproduce before the leaves come out.

But the hammock doesn't really have a temperate climate. The seasons that affect its organism most aren't winter, spring, summer, and fall, but a dry season running from October to May and a rainy season from June to September. Because of the many evergreen trees shading its floor, and the relatively dry conditions, April isn't "spring" in the hammock any more than it is a few dozen miles south where many tropical trees, like gumbo limbo and strangler figs, have their northernmost natural occurrence. (Cape Canaveral might be part of Yucatán, the Space Center towers thrusting like Mayan temples above hammocks of ebony and nakedwood.)

I wasn't satisfied with the hammock's subtropical self; I wanted the best of temperate and tropical too. John Muir expressed a similar dissatisfaction. "In visiting Florida in dreams of either day or night," he wrote, "I always came suddenly to a close forest of trees, every one in flower, and bent down and entangled to network by luxuriant and bright-looking vines and over all a flood of bright sunlight. But that was not the gate by which I entered the promised land. Salt marshes, belonging more to sea than land, with groves here and there, green and unflowered . . . In the dense Florida forests, sunlight cannot enter. In many places, there is not light sufficient to feed a single green leaf on those dark forest floors. All that the eye can reach is just a maze of tree stems and crooked, leafless vine strings. All the flowers, all the verdure, all the glory is up in the light."

Muir carried his dissatisfaction to metaphysical extremes. After surviving his malaria-ridden Florida visit, he concluded that "man . . . was never intended for such deadly climates" and speculated that God had created tropical forest to frustrate human attempts to conquer nature.

For someone with Muir's enormous insight into nature to feel thus shows how ingrained is the curious human dissatisfaction with real, earthly life. We've become like the birds that prefer incubating giant, artificial eggs to real ones. We respond to exaggerations of instinctual patterns more than to real ones, and thus we tend to bypass the relationships those patterns evolved to perpetuate. The people who throng Disney World and the coastal condos, for example, are responding to an exaggerated tropical pattern — to palms, beaches, suntanned bodies. The pattern is an artifice of advertising and technology, but it speaks to real instincts for warmth, lushness, nakedness. Because it is exaggerated, it attracts something in us more than does the real, subtropical Florida of hammocks, savannas, and wetlands, the Florida that actually *produces* warmth, water, food, shelter.

This confusion seems another hint that the brain might evolve out of sync with the whole organism. The fact that birds also are capable of preferring the exaggerated artificial to the real suggests that it is a biological phenomenon as well as a cultural one. Of course, birds were not faced with a choice between real and artificial eggs before culture started making artificial eggs. Maybe this simply shows that they aren't very bright. But then, stupidity also seems an example of brain-organism desynchronization.

The Canopy

I TRIED TO pay more attention to what was actually going on the next time I went into the hammock. I took the new trail, since everything along my old route seemed to have died or disappeared. It was another hot morning, and humid. It had rained the day before. It rains during Florida's dry season, just not every day as during the rainy season.

As I got in among the big live oaks and magnolias, I began hearing unfamiliar whistling sounds in the treetops. I couldn't see any birds making them. I wondered if it was tree frogs, which I'd never actually heard singing in trees. Most temperate tree frogs usually sing on or near the ground; treetop-singing frogs are typical of the tropics, where many species breed in epiphytes and tree holes.

With my attention on the canopy instead of the ground, I realized that many of the trees were blooming. The ground was littered with fallen blossoms: waxy white and purple magnolia petals, tiny golden red bay bells, and slightly larger white globes of cabbage palmetto. I picked up a partly opened magnolia bud the size of a small banana, which even smelled like a banana. As I sniffed the bud, I came eye to eye with a spider standing on it.

The spider looked as though it had fallen from a tropical canopy. It was bright green, and although it seemed to be a jumping spider, a member of a large group of non-web-building spiders that pursue their prey with spectacular leaps, it didn't look like any jumping spider I'd ever seen. Those were stout and hairy, but this one was slender and glossy, like a jumping spider thoroughbred. I later found it was a lyssomanes, a kind of jumping spider that lives mainly in the tropics.

Most jumping spiders are colorful, but this one was gaudy. On its head was what appeared to be a golden crown studded with rubies. Six tiny slate blue eyes stood in a double row in front of the crown, and in front of them was another pair of eyes, deep glossy black, about three times as large. The spider reared its head back and looked me up and down with these black eyes, then leapt away with agility surprising even in a jumping spider. It seemed to vanish.

Looking where it might have landed, I discovered that the golden silk spiders hadn't disappeared after all — it was just that they were about a quarter the size they'd been in November. This was the new generation, slightly pale but otherwise exact miniatures of their parents, hairy leg joints and all, and they were spinning their webs on all the shrubs.

Like lyssomanes, golden silk spiders are mainly tropical. The songbirds calling among this exoticism seemed a little incongruous, because they were the same species I'd have heard in northern woods: cardinals, red-eyed vireos, Carolina wrens, ovenbirds, redstarts, and pugnacious parula warblers that unfailingly flew down to scold me when I imitated a tit-mouse in their territories. Yet many would migrate to Central or South America by fall. Nothing points up the difficulty of carving the planet into geographical ecosystems more than the songbirds that spend their lives vacillating between temperate and tropical. It's as though they've lost permanent homes in some prehistoric habitat (perhaps the subtropical forest that once grew on today's deserts and grasslands) and have been wandering ever since.

My neck was getting stiff from craning at the treetops, so I was glad to come to a down-to-earth turtle in the path. It was a musk turtle, but it had yellow stripes on its head unlike the stinkpots in the sinkhole. I looked it up in my reptile book, which told me that there are two species of musk turtle in Florida and also that they have a reputation for falling out of trees onto people's heads. They like to sun on branches over streams, and leap before they look when startled by passing canoes. The turtle in the path, however, didn't do anything more acrobatic than pull into its shell.

The birds and frogs shut up as the sun ascended, and a rather oppressive silence had descended when I came to a swamp I hadn't seen before. It was right on the edge of the saw grass marsh, so it was even wetter than the palmetto swamp. A luxuriant welter of ferns, lilies, maiden canes, liverworts and other greenery grew under the red cedars and palmettoes. Even the water was covered with tiny floating duckweeds, as though the place was draped with green velvet. When I thrust a stick into the tannin-black water filling a rotten palmetto stump, it went down two feet before touching anything solid.

Yet for all its luxuriance, the swamp seemed utterly devoid of animal life except for the inescapable flies and mosquitoes. There was no sound or sight of birds, turtles, frogs . . . not even a vulture circling overhead. When I diluted the black, brackish water into translucence, I didn't find the evolutionary continuum of hydras, worms, rotifers, tiny crustaceans, mollusks, and amphibians that usually lives in sun-warmed shallows, but only fly and mosquito larvae. I supposed the salt and tannin in the water made it too corrosive for other creatures.

The swamp struck me as a redwood forest sometimes does, as though it had changed so little since the extinction of the dinosaurs that nothing else had been able to adapt to it. In the steamy noon, the glossy lily, palm, and fern leaves might have been made of jade rather than carbohydrates and chlorophyll. Trying to make some mental connection with such a place seemed about like trying to connect with a fossil forest buried under sixty million years of sedimentary rock.

The songbirds, spiders, and tree frogs up in the treetops seemed ephemeral epiphenomena compared to the swamp's green stoniness. This impression persisted as I walked back to the car without seeing or hearing an animal. The trees might have existed solely for the purpose of breeding tree-hole mosquitoes. I could understand why my recent ancestors had been in such a rush to cut them down.

Materialism

I FELT I'D struck a kind of rock bottom, what a materialist would expect at the heart of nature: an unyielding blankness beneath a thinnish crust of color and movement. It was like another version of the black hole that had panicked me in the western mountains, but not frightening, just wearing. The black hole in the mountains had been in me; this one seemed to have no more necessary connection to my consciousness than a pile of Paleozoic bones.

If the brain could so readily prefer the giant egg of artificial Florida to this, it suggested that there was no necessary evolutionary link between the brain and the forest after all, that they were two unnecessarily related complexes of molecules headed in different directions: the brain toward some genetically engineered future, the forest toward the frozen gene banks.

Yet I knew that this was superficial, that there are necessary molecular connections between forests and brains. Forests produce the oxygen which brains must burn to make the strange electrical discharges of consciousness. If our desires for artificial satisfactions seem independent of trees, it is only because our instinctual need to breathe has been so well pro-

97

vided for by many hundreds of millions of years of oxygen-making trees. Our conscious minds may remain blissfully unaware of this, but only until the oxygen is withdrawn.

The brain is a wayward enough organism to be dissatisfied with its own dissatisfaction. I couldn't accept the hammock's apparent vacancy. Alligators were supposed to bellow and carry on in spring mating season, not vanish. Several more mornings and afternoons on the mudbank only turned up the odd heron, however. I understood that creatures like wood storks were off mating elsewhere, but I'd never heard of alligators migrating. I wondered if they'd gone nocturnal. In the Okefenokee, a flashlight beam swept across midnight water had reflected in astonishing numbers of red eyes, each eye reflecting again in the water beneath it, but yellow this time, a very odd effect.

I decided I had to go in at night. If the kind of connections I was seeking in the brain existed, they were in the unconscious and the unconscious lives in the dark, figuratively, at least. I didn't know if rummaging in the literal dark would turn up anything from the figurative dark, but there didn't seem to be anything else to do.

When I went to get permission from the state park ranger, he was more suspicious than ever. I didn't know if he recognized me from two years before, but I hoped he didn't.

"Lots of mosquitoes and ticks in there now," he said.

"I know." I was starting to have trouble distinguishing the ticks attached to my skin from the scabs of previous bites.

"I was in there this morning. The deerflies are hatching out. They're *really* bad."

"Hm."

"I recommend you wear lots of insecticide if you go in there. In fact, take a bath in it."

I didn't think he really wanted me to bathe in malathion or aldrin and concluded he *was* given to careless usage. I took him at his meaning and wore a lot of repellent.

The Flies

I WENT INTO the hammock in the small hours, hoping the late night chill would quell the bugs. The stars were surprisingly bright for the low altitude, but the hammock didn't let any of their light in. It was pitch black, and dead silent. My breath billowed dankly in my flashlight beam.

After I'd walked awhile, I began to hear faint stridulations and feeble stirrings. Either it was getting warmer or my hearing was improving. Then I could see the white sand of the path. A cardinal called sleepily, a rooster crowed in the distance, and a chorus of frogs started somewhere. They sounded like big ranid frogs (the group that includes bullfrogs): they made a guttural, clattering noise.

A faint silhouette of palmetto tops marked the eastern horizon when I reached Bulow Creek. Misty clouds showed even more faintly above them. Nocturnal chuck-will's-widows (southern cousins of whippoorwills) still called in the marsh, but an early red-winged blackbird already bobbed and squealed on a cattail, although it was barely visible in the gray light.

The sky paled more quickly than I was used to in northern California. It made the dawn a little dreamlike, as though I was passing through a series of successively brighter rooms. First the western sky was a black wall, then a faint pattern of treetops, then a solid silhouette of leaves and branches. Cardinals started singing all along the creek as the last stars disappeared, and an osprey left its nest in the eastern treetops, flapped stiffly in the chill, then glided over the creek.

The creek water remained black despite the paling sky and exuded little eddies of gray vapor. Another line of mist rose on the far side of the marsh, indicating that there was another creek channel over there. Fish began to feed with startling snaps, and a chuck-will's-widow called so close that I could tell the "chuck" of its first cry from the "whip" sound of a whippoorwill.

Redness appeared in the east among snatches of cloud that apparently hadn't moved since my arrival. A train rumbled past to the west, and somebody revved a sports car hard on the state highway. At least, it sounded like a sports car the first time I heard it. The second time, I realized it was coming from the spike rushes right across the ditch from me instead of the highway: a deep, resonant growl with a menacing overtone.

I glanced behind me, checking escape routes, but the spike rushes remained motionless. Bartram had described alligators bellowing in the evening, but not growling in the morning. I didn't know what else in the marsh could make such a deep-throated noise. I wondered if it was growling at the train, which had shaken the ground, perhaps a disturbance to a sleeping alligator. Maybe it growled every morning as the train passed, like Pogo's friend Albert throwing his alarm clock out the window. On the other hand, perhaps it was growling at me. I held my breath, and there was another growl, but still no movement.

Then it was full daylight. A frenzied whistling issued from the treetops, so many birds singing at once that it was impossible to distinguish calls. A kingfisher darted out of the ditch mouth, probably from a nest burrow in the sandbanks upstream, and spotted sandpipers picked over sandbars next to small crabs that sidled out of the water. A large crab swam into sight in the creek at my feet, nibbling on a small one.

The east faded, then flushed again as the sun rose. A cardinal flew to the tip-top of a tree and sang at the red ball as though celebrating the cardinality of creation, but the sun quickly turned yellow and the cardinal flew away. The creek mist eddied faster in the warming air. A green heron landed on a snag upstream, and another landed on one downstream. They looked glum, like arriving office workers. A Louisiana heron joined the one upstream, which made as if to fly away, but didn't.

The treetop songbirds' excitement had abated, as though they'd sat down at their desks to start the day's paperwork. A barred owl hooted in a managerial sort of way, and a yellow-billed cuckoo made gulping sounds, as though visiting the water cooler. The air quickly went from warm to hot, and the marsh settled down to another day of somnolence. There evidently were alligators in it, but not confiding ones at present.

I started walking out and encountered organisms that made the growling alligator seem inoffensive. A big, whitish fly began buzzing around my head, so fast and loud that I forgot the mosquitoes. Every few seconds, it stopped buzzing, and I knew it had landed on me. It didn't land on my face or hands as a mosquito would have; it seemed to know where my blind spots were, hard-to-reach places like the backs of the legs. I couldn't just slap at it; I had to wheel around or flail myself with my hat. I tried flailing the fly, but it seemed to know about hats too. I began to get a little heated.

Then there were two big, whitish flies. I gave up flailing and ran a little way along the trail. Then there were three of them after me, and they sounded hungry, as though they'd been waiting a long time for something so succulent and defenseless to wander into the hammock. Paleontologists have speculated that biting insects helped drive some large Pleistocene mammals such as ground sloths into extinction. There had been a lot of ground sloths in the hammock's part of Florida eight thousand years before. In the Volusia County Museum, I'd seen the skeleton of one that had been dug out of a gravel pit along with platter-size fossil clams. The flies seemed about right for an eight-foot-tall beast.

I waited for the pain of a bite, but it didn't come, which wasn't altogether reassuring. Instead of tabanid flies, the bloodsucking flies usually known as horseflies and deerflies, these flies might be botflies of some kind. Botflies don't bite—they leave their eggs on their victims, and the maggots burrow into the skin. I ran again, farther this time, and they caught me, faster. Now there were four of them.

I started just running. I blundered into spiderwebs and stumbled over roots and cursed and panted like the jungle movie character who flees, cursing and panting, from army ants, but whose picked bones Charlton Heston later discovers anyway. I made it back to the sand road, however, and the flies sped away on the breeze, leaving me still waving my arms. I was glad the ranger wasn't watching.

Discomfort

I REMEMBERED flies from the western mountains. Insects generally aren't a great problem there because of the dry summers, but when I'd undergone spells of vertigo the flies had become nefarious. They were just houseflies and bluebottle flies for the most part, but their crawling and buzzing had seemed increasingly aggressive, almost as though they'd sensed some weakness, some hint of death or decay in the air around me.

Flies can seem an embodiment of the blank, stony face of nature, buzzing excitedly around carrion or excrement, reducing dead flesh to bone. Human dissatisfaction with life has no more vivid focus than a great crawling swarm of flies and maggots: they can make it seem hell on earth.

I'd gotten only a mild taste of Florida flies compared to what Audubon and Muir must have undergone. Even Bartram, who stayed much longer in Florida, called the flies "evil spirits . . . persecuting demons." "We travelled almost from sun-rise to his setting," he wrote, "amidst a flying host of these persecuting spirits, who formed a vast cloud around our caravan so thick as to obscure every distant object . . . whenever we approach the cool shades near creeks . . . we are surprised and quickly invested with dark clouds."

Yet Bartram, with an unusual tendency to look on the bright side of things, also admired the "splendid" colors of the flies that tormented him. This brings up a phenomenon that often struck me in the hammock. It wasn't really the sight of the flies, mosquitoes, and ticks that offended me; even the buzzings wouldn't have been so unpleasant if they hadn't been associated with the skin-crawling anticipation of bites. Much as we dislike flies, the fact is that they mainly offend one of our senses, touch. This is true of our relationship to the natural world in general. I saw, heard, or smelled unpleasant things in the hammock only occasionally, but I usually experienced some unpleasant tactile sensation: night chill, noon heat, sweat or insect itch. It's surprising how separated touch can be from other senses. I could feel leprous and suffocated from the humidity, and still admire spider colors.

One could object that the hammock felt unpleasant simply because I wasn't used to living in it, because my skin wasn't toughened and my circulation wasn't adjusted to living outside. There would be truth in this, but my eyes, ears, and nose were not any more used to the hammock than my skin. Why did they find it so much more agreeable? One could reply that their enjoyment was educated and privileged, that I could enjoy the hammock aesthetically because I didn't have to live there all the time. Yet people who live in hammocks all the time have been known to enjoy them.

The peculiar dualism of touch and the other senses seems a very large part of the dissatisfaction we feel with nature. The paradise we seek in artificial edens is largely one of touch, and we often sacrifice visual or auditory beauty to material comfort. To some extent, history has been an attempt to banish unpleasant sensations such as wetness and cold, and our prevailing myth of progress rests to a considerable extent on a hope that without these, we will be satisfied.

Older myths are more ambiguous and suggest that dissatisfaction arises less from discomfort than from the awareness of it, as with Adam and Eve's discovery of their naked vulnerability to fly bites and other things. This seems consistent with modern psychology, which sees the neocortex, with its ability to connect between discomfort that is and discomfort that is not yet (in other words, to plan), as the source of dissatisfaction and its attendant anxieties.

Dissatisfaction can seem the ultimate evidence of evolutionary unfitness between human organism and natural ecosystems, with the brain as a lever to pry them apart in a series of anxiety-driven feedback mechanisms. The more we try to abolish discomfort, the more sensitive to it we become, so it seems the brain has simply outgrown its physical environment and not only can, but must, turn it into something more suitable. Our ancestors fled the discomforts of tropical heat to the discomforts of temperate cold, and now we burn the very ground beneath our feet to reproduce tropical heat in our houses, or flee back to tropical heat, where we burn more coal and oil to reproduce temperate cold in our houses.

Yet it remains mysterious that the rest of our senses — sight, hearing, smell, even taste — are on the whole so pleasant. If an overgrown brain alienates from nature, why isn't the alienation felt overall? Why doesn't a swamp look and sound hideous in addition to its feeling damp, muggy, itchy? Of course, swamps do look hideous to some, but swamp-haters tend to like things like cathedrals which, art historians say, reflect the swampy forests of gothic Europe with their vaulting columns and buttresses.

Instead of alienation from nature, the complexity of our visual, auditory, and olfactory senses implies an evolving connection to the complexity of natural ecosystems. Pleasure is more complex than discomfort. Evolution builds enormously sophisticated forms and behaviors with pleasure. The flower is an example. With discomfort, evolution is more conservative, content to seal the organism in skin and a few variations thereof: scales, feathers, fur. Even these protective rudiments get preempted and elaborated for pleasure, as feathers become plumes for attracting sexual partners.

Discomfort tells of threats to the organism, and the brain obligingly, if unreliably, plans to deal with the threats. What pleasure tells the organism, and what the brain does with that information, seems much less straightforward.

The Armadillos

MY PREDAWN expedition had been unusually un-successful. The darker it had been, the less I'd perceived, which was normal for human consciousness, but not much of a start for getting at the unconscious. I wondered if the hammock had been so quiet, and my brain so numb, because it had been so chilly. I decided to go in just before sunset, when it was still hot and the animals (including, presumably, big whitish flies) were active.

It hadn't rained for a while, and some of the swampy places on the hammock's periphery had dried up. The air remained stiflingly humid. The only sounds in the late afternoon air were made by some gray squirrels rattling around in the canopy, and by the big whitish fly which promptly joined me. I ignored it, hoping it would go away. In a little while it did go away, perhaps disappointed by my failure to produce at-tractively irritated smells.

The golden silk spiders were noticeably bigger, and despite increased contact with the larger webs, I was feeling better about them, likely devourers of big whitish flies. At least, the webs seemed promising flytraps, the centers doubled to almost pillow thickness, the supporting threads like minia-ture cables, although I didn't see any trapped flies. I saw one spider eating a wasp, a reversal of the usual order, in which wasps feed spiders to their larvae.

The spiders weren't the only ones visibly growing. Swarms of jet black, yellow-striped lubber grasshoppers in grassy spots had been a half-inch long a few weeks before. Now they were an inch long. I wondered how big they'd be in August.

The sun set as I got to the drainage ditch. A layer of golden light ascended to the canopy, turned pink, then faded. The forest floor seemed brighter without it. As though stimulated by this, cicadas began a buzzing that rose to a shriek, then abruptly faded. The chirps and clicks of tree crickets and shield-backed grasshoppers became audible, and I again heard the ranid frogs in their hidden swamp, a clattering roar that rose and fell. It sounded powerful in the heat, and ominous. The swelling volume implied predatory expectation, even though it actually meant sexual anticipation.

I didn't hear alligator bellows, or even growls, and when I struggled out to the creek it was as vacant as ever, without even a heron. I might have waited until it was quite dark to see if the alligators came out, but it didn't seem such a good idea. Not only was sitting with alligators in the dark less appealing than sitting in daylight with them, but the creek was some distance from the trail, and I anticipated enough trouble keeping to the trail in the dark.

I returned to the trail and followed it in the direction of the jade swamp. It ran mainly through sand pine scrub, although there was one piece that seemed more lush. The ranid frog calls might have been coming from there, but they'd stopped by the time I passed it, and I didn't leave the trail to investigate. The light was failing fast.

A tiny, almost colorless flash caught my eye: a firefly. Underbrush noises were getting increasingly strange as the twilight deepened. Hundreds of tiny objects pattered from the treetops with a sound like fine rain. I shone my flashlight on the ground, but couldn't see what they were. As I switched on the light, something galloped away with a great thumping and crashing, but I couldn't see it either.

I came to a tongue of marsh that bordered the jade swamp, and the dull violet sky almost dazzled me after the dimness under the trees. Tree frogs called along the swamp edge, and a chuck-will's-widow started up out in the marsh. Fireflies multiplied, first in the tree shadow, then over the marsh as the sky darkened. By the time the stars came out, the marsh was wired with fireflies flashing in pulses, like sophisticated Christmas tree lights. They were all tiny and pale, unlike the fat orange or green fireflies of northern meadows, and they flashed so briefly that the effect was feverish, like heat lightning. They made the night seem darker.

The abrupt nightfall changed my mood. In the twilight I'd been intrigued by strange noises: now they unnerved me. I'd wanted a lively night, but this seemed a bit too much too soon, especially since I couldn't see what was making the noises. I jumped as another thump and rustle sounded near my feet. I turned the flashlight on it, but the underbrush was motionless, as though nothing had ever been there.

Insect calls now sounded furtive. Long calls like the cicadas' had given way to short and ventriloquial ones. The fireflies separated their brief flashes with lengthy flights, flashing once near the treetops, then once or twice again during rapid descents. The only ones that stayed alight longer were a pair on the ground, perhaps mating. Fireflies flash to attract mates, although one predatory species imitates the flash patterns of other species and eats them when they approach.

The darkness deepened as I entered the jade swamp. It played tricks with space. I began mistaking fireflies for distant car headlights, flashlights or windows. The rising of an orange moon didn't dispel the confusion: it dazzled me and made the shadows darker. The fireflies seemed discouraged by the moonlight and flashed less, although one would occasionally flash in a moonbeam. It looked like a highlight on metal.

I finally discovered what was doing the thumping and rustling: armadillos. I was impressed, then appalled by their numbers as they grew increasingly bold. I started passing one every few yards, and they didn't gallop away anymore. They kept rummaging around my feet, like pushy shoppers. The hammock appeared infested with giant woodlice.

One armadillo was so unconcerned at my approach that it kept its head thrust into a hole it was investigating. I mistook it for a rock until I recalled that the sandy swamp didn't *have* rocks in it. I could have picked it up, and when it finally pulled its head out, it made no attempt to flee. It merely sneezed faintly and blinked in my flashlight beam, an improbable amalgam of sweet potato head, leathery flop ears, scaly sausage body, and hairy little trotters and tail. Its tiny eyes didn't shine in the light, suggesting that it had no night vision (a reflective membrane behind the retina of nocturnal animals gives them night vision). It probably found its way about by smell and sound.

Armadillos aren't native to modern Florida. A few that escaped from an animal show in the 1930s multiplied to occupy the state. I feared this exotic horde might pick the hammock clean of small native fauna, but then I reflected that a hundred thousand or so years ago, when hammocks were about the same ecologically as they are now, bulldozer-size ground sloths and Volkswagen-size glyptodonts (giant extinct relatives of armadillos) had occupied the area without eating everything.

I still found the armadillos slightly repellent in the darkness, although they'd seemed droll in daylight. They evoked a creeping sensation that seems latent to human flesh after dark. Their scuffling and snuffling had the itchy edge of a mosquito's whine. The harsh flashlight made them look baleful, and even the moonlight didn't prettify them, merely scissoring the woodlouse shapes with palmetto shadows. The damp earth they turned up smelled of musk and mold.

I felt a little as though I were an armadillo myself, a scuffling creature oblivious to color, sweetness, musicality. It seemed the opposite of the colorful, fragrant afternoon with the alligators, even though the armadillos were mammals like me. But then, primates are highly aberrant mammals in their diurnal habits, their liking for color. Most mammals like night as well as day, if not better.

It was past midnight, and the hammock was quieting down. The fireflies had all but disappeared, and the moon, now at zenith, penetrated the canopy less than it had in rising. It was darker than ever, and I was having the expected trouble following the path. Even with the flashlight, my eyes couldn't easily distinguish its beaten earth from the compacted leaf litter of the forest floor. It seemed to fork every few feet, and I strayed from it more than once when I mistook lichen patches or moonlight for the white blazes. Retracing my steps, I had to search carefully for marks I'd have noticed with a glance even in twilight.

I felt pressure behind my eyes. Panic waited there, ready to proclaim that not only had I lost the trail, but that the trail had never even been there, that my conscious life had been a dream from which the awakening was this darkness, this "land of oblivion." I was back with Audubon's lost one in the fog, my brain an apparent tabula rasa, without innate orientation. The patches of saw palmetto and tree trunks in my flashlight beam were the only proof of existence, and they all looked the same. If I lost the trail, I would circle in the mud until morning, because I couldn't even get directions from the stars.

Yet there did seem to be one innate reaction, peculiarly at odds with my educated anxieties. At the same time panic pressed behind my eyes, I could feel a drowsiness seeping into the back of my head. It was less noticeable than the anxiety, but just about as powerful, so that the two states alternated in my mind rather disconnectedly. One moment I'd be straining my eyes at the path, the next my eyelids would be drooping, and behind them I'd see flickers of the fugitive little scenes and dramas that the unconscious mind plays for the conscious one right at the border of sleeping and waking.

I heard things too, little whispers that might have been in the treetops or my head for all that my ears could make out of their origins. When an owl hooted from what sounded like a few feet from the trail, I was pretty sure *it* was real, but I still couldn't see it no matter how I shone the flashlight about.

It was about two A.M. when I got to the grassy track leading to where my car was parked. The night had stayed warm enough for insects, and I'd spent as much time looking for spiderwebs across the trail as I had for the trail. A face full of spiderwebs feels extraordinarily stifling in darkness. I thus succeeded in stopping an inch short of a spider even bigger than a golden silk, which had built an immense web across the track since sunset. It was an *Araneus* orb web weaver with an abdomen the size of a small plum and a web full of fat june beetles. *Araneus* orb weavers are supposed to retreat to rolled-leaf nests if disturbed, but this one didn't budge an inch as I shone the light on it—it just hung there before my nose, a silver pendant on the nocturnal bosom. I sidled around it.

Dreams

I'D SPENT a lot of time wandering around in the western mountains at night, so my experience in the hammock wasn't unexpected. I'd often heard fugitive treetop whisperings in the West, and I'd eventually found that flying squirrels were making them, animals that probably live in the hammock too, although I didn't see them there. I'd also experienced the abrupt alternation of anxiety and drowsiness. As I'd become more used to being in the dark woods, the drowsiness had come to dominate, and I'd become comfortable with simply lying down where I happened to be, without fire or sleeping bag if it was warm enough, and snoozing away. Nothing bad had happened despite the absence of the usual safeguards in which sleeping humans wrap themselves. It had felt liberating, like finding I could breathe underwater.

One way to avoid getting lost is to simply stay where you are, and falling asleep is a good way to do that. For the brain of a diurnal, tree-dwelling, fruit-eating creature like an ape to shut down automatically at night seems a sensible sort of mediation between organism and environment. Apes sensibly make tree nests and stay in them at night.

Of course, our human ancestors stopped sleeping in trees

as long as five million years ago. My ease at stretching out in the western mountains was greatly enhanced by the fact that no reliably man-eating predators lived there. The lion- and hyena-dominated savanna where human ancestors slept had no such advantages, yet our ancestors slept out in it without benefit of Land Rovers, tents, or even fire, in the case of the early australopithecines and *Homo habilis.*

That hominids have been evolving on the ground for mil- lions of years while retaining a nocturnal behavior more ap- propriate in the trees seems another example of evolution that doesn't solve problems, doesn't increase fitness. One would expect natural selection to have produced hominid populations with steadily improving nocturnal vision and other powers, yet the human organism continues to wilt like a poppy after sunset.

It's true that there has been cultural adaptation to our noc- turnal helplessness. Our ancestors apparently were building little rock and brush sleeping shelters fairly early, and fire was a big change. Yet these things didn't let us function bet- ter at night: they simply let us sleep through it more safely. In a sense, they perpetuated the human organism's noctur- nal helplessness.

Yet not all parts of the human organism go torpid at night. Like the nocturnal flowers that open to the visits of moths and bats when the plant's photosynthetic activity is dormant, the brain stays open to the strange consciousness of dreams. Unlike bats and moths, of course, dreams come from within the brain. Still, it's hard to understand just what function they perform for the whole organism. Freud thought dreams were a way of expressing anarchic desires, and modern physio- logists see them as factors of metabolic regulation. Dreams may play both roles, but I don't know if either theory can entirely explain them.

As with insanity, we don't really know what dreams are biologically. Their evolution will probably always be a mystery, at least with our present knowledge, although we can be pretty sure that higher animals experience both, as anyone knows who has observed a dreaming pet, or a crazy pet. At least insanity is abnormal. We can try to dismiss it as a biological malfunction, a chemical aberration. We can have no such reassurance with dreams.

If dreams have evolved to serve the organism, why are they so bizarre? Why don't we just dream of going about normal functions — eating, working, reproducing — instead of the witches' brews we consume at night? Perhaps dreams are bizarre simply because randomly excited neurons produce random association, crossing normal daytime memories to produce animal-headed people and other dream fare. Yet this doesn't explain to me the extraordinary power that dreams have to make their strangeness convincing. The brain dreams not only artifacts like animal-headed people, but entire environments of astonishing complexity and splendor, as when Coleridge based "Kubla Khan" not only on Bartram's *Travels* but on a particularly vivid and detailed dream which the book, and opium, had evoked.

It is really very odd that we can so vividly dream of flying, living underwater, becoming other animals or objects. What is the significance of this for a walking primate? What, on the other hand, might its significance be for a nerve cell colony packed with genetically coded information going back to long before primates walked, or even slept in the trees?

Many societies have considered dreams more significant, even more real, than waking life, which raises a question as to whether the organism might end up serving the organ. Flowering plants originated as woody trees or shrubs, if primitive angiosperms like magnolia are any indication, but the most recently evolved angiosperms are grasses and herbs — small, soft plants on which the flower tends to be proportionately much larger than on trees. There are functional reasons for this evolutionary trend — grasses and herbs can thrive in environments difficult for woody plants — yet specialized development of flowers seems too prevalent a theme to be ignored. Flower dominance reaches ultimate expression in the ephemeral, a very common type of plant which lives only long enough to flower and set seed.

The human brain isn't getting bigger in proportion to the organism, despite all the new things it does. But it is developing a lot of cultural specialization, and it has increasing power over the organism. It is interesting how much of this cultural specialization, from new religions to scientific discoveries, has stemmed from the dreams of exceptional individuals such as Coleridge. One might almost think that the brain was deliberately isolating itself in the darkness of the ape's sleeping cycle to further some cellular strategy of its own.

If the dreaming brain seems isolated from the organism, it might seem even more isolated from the environment, its sensory inputs closed by unconsciousness (although sounds, smells, and even sights of the sleeping organism do influence dreams). Dreams often seem to lead away from nature into fantasy, artificiality. Yet one might also see the dreaming brain as linked to the environment in time, even though separated in space. If the unconscious mind lives in a kind of eternity, then the waters and trees of the dream landscape could be more than the random reflections of the organism's waking experience. It would be interesting to know what a mind raised in complete environmental isolation would dream, and what unborn infants dream.

The Turkeys

UNNERVING as my nocturnal expeditions were, they revealed *something* that was going on in the hammock. Yet I didn't want to get sidetracked into the land of dreams and snuffling armadillo consciousness. It seemed premature, considering how little I understood about primate consciousness. Finding your way in the dark may be a dubious achievement if you're still getting lost in the daytime.

I gave up looking for two-year-old epiphanies and started simply going to the hammock when I felt like it. Predictably, when I stopped looking for things, I started finding things. They continued to be unexpected.

The hammock still refused to put on a vernal aspect. It didn't rain for a couple of weeks, and the vegetation began to look stressed. Trees seemed to be shedding epiphytes: brown sprigs of resurrection fern, shiny greenfly orchid leaves, and bulbous or spiky bromeliads littered the ground under the live oaks. Even the lichenlike Spanish moss seemed to be suffering, the green tissues of the plants sloughing off the black, horsehair-like skeletons. I wondered again if the winter's heavy frosts had affected the warm-weather plants.

Frosts may be increasing in Florida because much of the state's wetlands have been drained in the past two decades.

Water retains heat and cold longer than air, so wet places have smaller temperature fluctuations than dry places. I'd seen ice-covered puddles in Ormond Beach in December, but never in the swampy hammock. Wetlands don't figure largely in dream tropics, so Floridians plant drained and filled land with royal palms and orange trees which then die in frosts.

Orange trees had no trouble surviving in wilderness Florida. Introduced by the Spanish, they soon grew wild all over the peninsula, eliciting William Bartram's usual enthusiasm: "the pendant golden Orange dancing on the surface of the pellucid waters, the balmy air vibrating with the melody of the merry birds, tenants of the encircling aromatic grove . . . " Wild groves have been supplanted by commercial ones, but feral trees linger in hammocks. I'd seen some in fruit in Bulow Hammock two years before, spindly trees bearing a few fungus-blackened oranges.

I'd been looking for orange trees without success on this trip. The next time I went into the hammock, I found one right beside the trail, a moldy sapling ten feet tall with two frayed leaves near its top. I suppose I noticed it because the dry weather made the hammock look different. A vine-covered tree that had looked like something in Brazil in humid weather now looked like something in Connecticut, as though it wasn't the plants that made the hammock temperate or tropical, but the air that happened to be blowing through on any given day. Today's air probably was from Connecticut, or the North Atlantic, just as muggy air came from the Caribbean.

Animals seemed less sensitive to the weather than plants. The golden silk spiders kept growing, the green and pink ones had reappeared, and I found another golden-crowned lyssomanes jumping spider, as bouncy as the first. Lizards were more in evidence than ever, showing signs of breeding activity. Anoles puffed out scarlet throats, ground skinks squirmed across the leaf litter, race runners darted through glades, and a big five-lined skink rushed up a tree.

I passed a yellow corn snake at the periphery of the hammock, and a black racer further in. These were the only snake species I ever saw in the hammock. Despite my grandmother's warnings, the only poisonous snake I'd ever seen in the entire vicinity had been a diamondback rattlesnake which was, very unexpectedly, swimming the Tomoka River estuary at a place where it appeared at least a mile wide. It had seemed like a lot of snake at the time. It's hard to be objective about a diamondback rattlesnake, the largest North American snake, when the wind is blowing your canoe at one. The snake, which was probably not excessively large, had landed inoffensively on the shore of Tomoka State Park and disappeared into the brush.

I came to the part of the hammock where the biggest trees grew, not only ancient live oaks but ashes and hickories with bark like elephant skin and tropical-looking buttresses. The ground was swampy under these water-loving species, with little rivulets meandering through lush patches of grass and cane. As I was stepping across a rivulet, I heard a faint noise behind me.

I turned and saw a hen turkey sneaking away into some magnolia saplings. I'd walked right past her. She didn't make another sound as she moved out of sight. I glimpsed another hen a little farther off.

The turkeys evidently knew I'd seen them, because they began to make squawking, gulping sounds as soon as they were safely invisible. Suddenly, a smaller bird rocketed out of a patch of grass and ferns a few yards from me, unloading a squirt of excrement before it disappeared into the branches of the subcanopy. When I focused my binoculars on the patch, I saw the heads of several more turkey chicks protruding from it. They began to mill around and peep, probably frightened by the giant black eyes of the binocular lenses. I expected them to break cover and fly away too, as grouse and quail probably would have.

Instead, the hens did something I'd never seen. They came back and collected the chicks. Both reemerged from the safety of the saplings, still clucking, and within seconds they had led the chicks out of sight. It seemed surprisingly calm, deliberate behavior for birds related to chickens. A bobwhite quail family I'd stumbled on near Cape Canaveral had become so excited that not only the parents but one of the *chicks* had put on a broken wing act.

The turkeys' disappearance was so swift and complete that the effect was spectral. I examined the grassy patch for a sign of the chicks' presence, but found not a feather. Even the excrement the one chick had dropped seemed to have disappeared. I didn't see turkeys in the hammock again: it was as though they inhabited a realm only fitfully accessible to me. I could see why they fascinated the ranger.

The hammock relapsed into its afternoon torpor after the turkeys disappeared, the whine of mosquitoes broken only by the occasional hammerings of distant woodpeckers. Yet the birds' abrupt manifestation, like something in a fun house, made the hammock seem made of a green glass rather than jade. The tedium I'd felt in my earlier daytime visits changed to the expectancy one feels when something that had been opaque begins to clear.

The trouble with glass is that it can be reflective as well as transparent. It can seem to show the inside of things while it is only showing the outside. Finding my way in a hammock of glass didn't seem all that much more promising than finding my way in a hammock of stone, although it did seem more interesting.

Reflections

THE TURKEYS' fun house appearance brought up the aspect of the brain that I find most mysterious: its enormous capacity for mimicry. Even simple perceptions — sight, hearing, smell, touch — are forms of mimicry, wherein the brain produces a kind of electro-cellular imitation of the phenomena which eyes, ears, nose, and skin transmit to it. When the organism sees something, it is really seeing an interior projection, a kind of mirror image.

Perception is a large enough can of worms. Things get *really* mysterious, however, when behavior is involved. Then the brain in effect takes the imitations of environment, which perceptions are, and projects them not only back onto the organism, but onto the environment as well. Organisms not only see and hear parts of the environment, they imitate them. Young birds imitate their parents' movements and calls. Some birds imitate calls and movements of other bird species. Some birds (and many other organisms) imitate the appearance of other species. From such transactions issues the entire spectrum of human behavior: learning, culture, art, science, technology, and that ultimate solar imitation, the thermonuclear explosion.

Humans can't really be said to have inherited our talent for mimicry from birds, since we are mammals. Yet, our ancestors having been first treetop animals, then two-legged ground-dwelling ones, we inhabit a sensory world rather more like the average bird's than the average mammal's. As primates, we are old-fashioned mammals, closer to the tree-hopping gnomes of fifty million years ago than to dogs or cows, and thus closer to the dinosaur age of which the birds seem to be the most significant survivors.

I suppose this is why so many people feel a sense of affinity and recognition with birds. Our admiration for their bright colors, sweet songs, and graceful flight suggests that some very large part of our brains is still up in the canopy with them, surrounded by insects that look like flowers and flowers that look like insects. Even millions of years after descending from the tropical forest canopy, the hominid brain continues to seek its elevated qualities in environments, and to reproduce them artificially in hundreds of ways, from the highs of drug intoxication to the giant eggs of tourist Florida.

Another quality of birds that we admire is their ability to find their way across vast distances without benefit of maps, roads or any other travel aids. Newly fledged birds are quite capable of migrating halfway across the planet, and we still don't understand how they do it. Even the nonmigratory turkeys I met in the hammock seemed to have a mysterious orientation in the environment, as evidenced by their elusive-ness. Turkeys are stupid birds in captivity, but in the wild they are very hard to catch.

I wondered if the brain's talents for mimicry might extend to some kind of innate mapping or orientation system, a system that mammals might share, although perhaps to a lesser degree, with birds. Could each brain contain, perhaps buried somewhere, perhaps atrophied, a kind of cellular model of the planet that would allow the organism to move across large, unknown portions of it in a purposeful way? Obviously, this would be impossible if the brain was a tabula rasa, but the brain obviously is not one. It recently has been likened to a new scientific concept of the immune system. Instead of learning to make antibodies *after* pathogens invade the organism, it now appears that the immune system contains innate genetic codes that match the molecular structures of disease organisms. In effect, the system *knows* the disease organisms before it encounters them. The brain may contain similar genetic codes that allow it to respond to a wide variety of environmental cues in unconscious and automatic ways. As bird migration indicates, some of these behaviors could be impressively complex. And birds have small brains. What might be the implications of such behaviors ramified through the relatively enormous hominid brain?

Of course, infant humans don't go wandering off across the continents as fledgling birds do. The range of innate human behavior seems feeble by comparison with birds: we do most things from learning. But who is to say that learning might not be masking some innate potentials? Humans actively try to mask innate potentials that don't fit with accepted cultural standards, and have been doing so for a long time. Moving from the tropics to the no-nonsense temperate zones, we humans have tried at various times to suppress our curiosity, our love of color, our playfulness, our roving sexual appetites. Perhaps we lost some innate spatial orientation with the environment we had evolved in, rather as we left behind some of the disease organisms to which our immune systems were adjusted.

It would be easy to dismiss ideas of the brain mimicking ancestral environments if all the Europeans who came to places like Florida had viewed them with the bewilderment and alarm of Audubon and Muir. This was the normal reaction, but it wasn't the only one. There was William Bartram, who was in Florida when it was still Indian territory, and suffered much more there than either Muir or Audubon, but who stayed more than a year, wandering in a sort of rapture, as though in an earthly paradise.

As I've said, William Bartram is a mystery. An easygoing, impractical personality, he might have been expected to respond to his plantation debacle in Picolata, his year of hunger and illness alone with six slaves, by keeping well clear of Florida. Instead, after returning to Philadelphia, working as a farmhand, then going bankrupt in business and leaving town to escape debtor's prison, he headed right back to the peninsula with an assignment to collect specimens for a rich Englishman.

In the *Travels,* his account of that trip, there is barely a hint of bewilderment or alarm, despite some terrifying experiences, but rather a way of perceiving the natural world that had little historical precedent. When his father, John, had described a Florida sinkhole spring in 1766, it had smelled "like bilge," tasted "sweetish and loathsome" and boiled up from the bottom "like a pot." Ten years later, William described a quite similar spring as an "enchanting and amazing crystal fountain, which incessantly threw up, from rocky caverns below, tons of water every minute . . . the blue ether of another world." These are such different ways of seeing that one wonders how they evolved within a single generation. William certainly wasn't influenced by romanticism, since he preceded it and partly caused it. He read eighteenth-century nature poetry, but so did his father. Seminole culture also influenced him, but it seems doubtful he could have described it as sympathetically as he did (his father disliked Indians) without acquiring a new vision first.

I'm not the only one who's been puzzled at Bartram's unprecedented raptures. Audubon, among others, simply decided that "Mr. Barton" was a liar. Yet most of Bartram's observations have been upheld scientifically, and even his stranger outbursts can have a ring of authenticity. Thomas Carlyle saw in his "floundering eloquence" a "future Biblical article." The novelist James Branch Cabell confessed to a grudging suspension of disbelief at Bartram's radically Rousseauian vision of a naked Seminole who "reclines and reposes under the odiferous shades of Zanthoxylon, his verdant couch guarded by the Deity; Liberty and the Muses inspiring him to wisdom and valor whilst the balmy zephyrs fan him to sleep."

"One inclines . . . to shrug off the whole matter," Cabell wrote, "as a high-flown invention of the 'noble savage' school of romance. Yet one would thus miss the main, the perplexing point of these rhapsodies . . . which is, that William Bartram was never a liar. The man was, instead, painstakingly truthful. In his exact, unbiased, and microscopic facility for observation he was excelled by no person then living. One confronts here, in brief, an enigma which, it can but be repeated, has no known solution."

The Springs

I WAS GETTING restless with the hammock again. Bartram hadn't passed all his rapturous wandering in a single little patch of woods. He'd seen vast open spaces like the Alachua Savanna or apparently bottomless sinkholes full of "innumerable bands of fish . . . some clothed in the most brilliant of colors." The savanna hadn't reflected much of the glory when I'd been there, so I decided to go to a spring.

The nearest one to Bulow Hammock was Ponce de León Springs near Deland, which John James Audubon also visited during his Bulow sojourn. He set out for it, then called Spring Garden Plantation, a few days after the pelican-collecting debacle on the Halifax. John Bulow again accompanied him, perhaps trying to make up for the previous unpleasantness.

Things went better this time, eventually. "The weather was pleasant, but not so our way . . . It seemed to us as if we were approaching the end of the world. The country is perfectly flat, and, as far as we could survey it, presented the same wild and scraggy aspect . . . disagreeable journey." After a night at the plantation, however, "our amiable host" showed them "the way to the celebrated spring, the sight of which afforded me a pleasure sufficient to counter-balance the tediousness of my journey . . . a circular basin, having a diameter of about sixty feet, from the center of which water is thrown up with great force . . . a kind of whirlpool is formed . . . on the edges of which are deposited vast quantities of shells, with pieces of wood, gravel, and other substances which have coalesced into solid masses having a curious appearance."

Ponce de León Springs became a private resort during the Florida vacation boom of the early twentieth century. My parents had taken me there in the 1950s. As with the hammock, the state of Florida saved it from becoming developed into condominiums by buying it in the 1980s. When I returned in 1984, I found the place little changed from the 1950s, with the same fancy stucco gate, wide lawns, spreading oaks, peacocks — same promoter's antebellum reverie. It still compared favorably to the ranks of houses that would have been its fate under corporate development.

The spring was the same too: a circular, cemented swimming pool walled with bathhouses. (The Coke machine was new.) A mild ebullience still emerged from the gravel bottom at the center of the pool, but the "great force" Audubon had described had long ago dissipated into the bathtubs and toilets of the nearby town. When I took a swim, the water was still crystal clear. A few small fish had gotten in somehow.

Most of Florida's sinkhole springs have suffered fates similar to Ponce de León's, and even where they haven't been concreted over, their native fish populations have been decimated. Yet there's still something extraordinary about them. The water remains "pellucid" as Bartram called it, strikingly clear. It seems to exhilarate fish: they jump unusually often and high in it. There's a kind of aura over spring runoff, a charged feeling, so that it seems right to find fantastic beasts like manatees in it, as they can still be found in the spring John Bartram called "sweetish and loathsome." Manatees winter in springs because the water is warmer than in lakes and rivers, a prosaic enough reason, but they look mythical wallowing like obese, freckled mermen in an outflow channel hardly wider than their body length.

I took a canoe out on Spring Garden Lake, into which Ponce de León Springs flows. The lake connects with the marshes of Lake Woodruff National Wildlife Refuge, and then with the St. Johns River, an area where Bartram was at his most exultant in the *Travels*. It seemed as likely a place as any to glimpse something of his vision. There is even a small national wilderness area, one of the few in Florida outside the Everglades.

It's exhilarating to push off into big swampland, and it was particularly so in the springwater, which remained so clear for many yards from shore that I could see bass hovering above the waterweeds as though in air. A chorus of croaks, snaps, gurgles and splashes carried crisply from rafts of water lettuce and hyacinth along the shore. Boat-tailed grackles and purple gallinules strutted across the floating leaves. Every few yards I'd pass a larger bird, with brown and white speckled plumage and long, curved bill, which would absentmindedly let me drift close enough to almost touch it. These were limpkins, odd tropical wading birds confined to Florida swamps in the United States and threatened by their tameness and sensitivity to water pollution. I'd seen few limpkins in the area the decade before, but their population was up now because their main food, the apple snail, was more numerous.

Audubon managed to shoot two limpkins during an unstranded boat expedition from Spring Garden Plantation to the St. Johns, and it briefly raised his estimation of Florida. Limpkins in hand, he "landed on a small island covered with wild orange trees, the luxuriance and freshness of which were not less pleasing to the sight, than the perfume of the flowers to the smell . . . amidst the golden fruits that covered the ground, while humming birds flutterd over our heads, we spread our cloth on the grass, and with a happy and thankful heart I refreshed myself with the bountiful gifts of an ever-careful providence."

Bartram had a harder time in the vicinity. Camped in an orange grove by the water, he took his boat out to fish for supper and was "attacked on all sides" by alligators, "several endeavoring to upset the canoe . . . They struck their jaws together so close to my eyes as almost to stun me, and I expected any moment to be dragged out of the boat and instantly devoured." He beat them off with a club and returned to camp, where another alligator attacked him. He shot it. Then, as he bent over the water to clean his fish, *another* alligator that had been hiding underwater almost grabbed him.

This might have seemed enough adventure for a dozen expeditions, but no sooner had Bartram dragged his gear away from the alligator-dominated shore and cooked his fish than "two very large black bears" appeared on a direct course for his dinner. He managed to drive *them* away, but the "tumultuous noise" of the alligators kept him awake most of the night, and they attacked him again as he pushed off in the morning. He had camped at a breeding and feeding concentration of bull alligators: he described a line of them stretching across the river to intercept migrating fish.

By the next evening, a continuing alligator turmoil "had almost deprived me of every desire but that of ending my troubles as speedily as possible . . . I was awakened and greatly surprised, by the terrifying screams of owls in the deep swamps around me, and what increased my extreme misery was the difficulty of getting quite awake, and yet hearing at the same time such screaming and shouting, which increased and spread every way for miles around, in dreadful peals . . . " Finally rousing himself, Bartram discovered yet *another* alligator "dashing my canoe against the roots of a tree, endeavoring to get into her for the fish."

John James Audubon's response to these experiences would have been predictable. I suppose mine would have been, too: they were just the thing to bring on night sweats, dizzy spells, and a craving for beachfront condos. Yet the night of the alligators came toward the *beginning* of Bartram's Florida sojourn (they would bellow in his dreams for the rest of his life), and his tolerance was highly unusual.

He kept right on up the St. Johns, through a hurricane that destroyed most of the plantation he'd set out to visit. He survived the storm by hanging on to bushes while sitting in his flooded canoe by the riverbank. When he returned downriver a few days later, he had this to say about the "deep swamps" that had so persistently been trying to kill him: "How harmonious and soothing is this native sylvan music now at still evening! . . . this is indeed harmony, even amidst the incessant croaking of the frogs: the shades of silent night are made more cheerful with the shrill voice of the whip-poor-will and active mockbird . . . What a beautiful display of vegetation is here before me! seemingly unlimited in extent and variety: how the dew drops twinkle and play upon the sight, trembling on the tips of the lucid green savanna, sparkling as the gem that flames on the turban of the eastern prince. See the pearly tears rolling off the buds of the expanding Granadilla: behold the azure fields of cerulean Ixea! . . . What a beautiful retreat is here! Blessed, unviolated spot of earth."

Canoeing in Bartram's wake, I couldn't help feeling I was missing something. The *water* was still there, that was something. It was nice to see limpkins, swallowtail kites, the odd alligator. Yet the vegetation was so utterly different from what Bartram described as to make me feel half blind. Not only were there no "expanding" passionflowers or "azure fields" of wild iris, the very "high forests and orange groves," the "vast cypress swamps" that formed the background of Bartram's "poems" (as Coleridge called his descriptions) had disappeared, logged off in the early twentieth century. The low expanse of red maple swamp that had succeeded them reminded me more of Canadian muskeg than earthly paradise.

Away from the spring, the lake water turned a dull tannic brown, slicked with oil. There was no mystery about where that came from. I'd have been glad of a few alligator growls in exchange for the outboards that started roaring past me full of fishermen every few minutes. The few smallish alligators along the banks seemed to know better than to compete with the din, slipping into the water with a kind of resigned furtiveness as I passed.

Hoping for a little peace, I ran up a small creek in the national wildlife refuge. According to my map, it was inside the wilderness area, off limits to motorboats, but no sooner had I tied up to a snag than a really incredible roar erupted. I though an airplane was about to crash on me.

Instead, an airboat sped around the bend. When it came abreast, the two men in it turned the propeller down enough to ask me if I'd seen another airboat. I answered that I wouldn't have needed to *see* it, but I don't think they heard me. They put their ear protectors back on and roared away, leaving a wake so high I was surprised it didn't tear the saw grass off the bank.

Yet there was still a hint of glory in the place as I paddled back in the evening. Saw grass and water stretched to every horizon, and the marshland seemed more than real estate, as though the brimming water table had suffused it with an indestructible substrate of vitality. Herons fishing in Spring Garden Creek stood their ground when I passed, confident of possession, and a tree full of black vultures let me get close enough to be startled by the clapping of their wings. They eyed me timidly. A raccoon at the water's edge ignored me completely. The sun had set when I got back to the spring outlet, but I could still see the bottom.

The Tortoise

CONSIDERING how little remained of William Bartram's Florida, I didn't see how I could get much insight into the extraordinary rapport he had established with it. Wilderness Florida could very well have evoked some innate potential in his brain, but the prospects for mine seemed less promising. Even birds have trouble migrating nowadays; they wind up banging into high-rises and jetliners. I doubted if I could even succeed in getting lost in the Daytona vicinity: there'd always be a jeep trail or sand road to stumble on.

I kept going back to the hammock anyway and made a few discoveries. I figured out the difference between cabbage palmetto and saw palmetto. Since cabbage palmetto is a tree and saw palmetto a shrub, I had been assuming that any shrub palmetto was a saw palmetto and any tree palmetto was a cabbage palmetto. Then it dawned that cabbage palmetto had to undergo a shrubby sapling stage. I'd begun to feel dull frustration every time I saw a shrubby palmetto. The leaves all looked the same.

Suddenly one morning, I found that I had looked at enough palmetto leaves to be able to distinguish the two species. In fact, their leaves were so different that I could hardly believe I'd had trouble telling them apart. Saw palmetto's palmate fronds grow tidily from the tip of the leaf stem, while cabbage palmetto's grow along the last few inches of the stem, giving the leaves a clumsy aspect.

It wasn't much of a discovery, in fact it was embarrassing, but it made the hammock a little less petrified and glassy. It was a breezy day, so the vegetation seemed more animated than usual. The mosquitoes were also more inhibited. This may have sharpened my vision, because I soon made another discovery.

In a glade where the grass grew thick along the trail, I came upon a gopher tortoise. I had no trouble identifying *it*. It was three times as large as the stinkpots, with a high-domed carapace, square head, and elephantine feet. Yet it was more timid than the smaller turtles, visibly cringing as I approached. Tortoises can't stink, snap, or otherwise repel humans, and their meat is palatable, as the ranger had told me.

It's a little surprising that tortoises have survived in the clever-pawed mammalian world, although fossils show they evolved at about the time the dinosaurs disappeared. Their slowness may be exaggerated. Indeed, instead of withdrawing into its shell as I passed, this tortoise snapped out its legs and took off down the trail at a brisk trot. It disappeared in the grass, headed for its burrow, I supposed. Gopher tortoise burrows can extend thirty-five feet underground, a factor that may have something to do with the species' survival. Tortoises were thriving in Bartram's day. He found the burrows in "great numbers" and likened them to "vast caves . . . castles . . . casting out incredible quantities of earth."

A deer snorted in the bushes, then several does fled noisily, waving their white flags. Deer seemed bolder than they had two years before, but that had been during hunting season. I paused beside a cabbage palmetto leaf and saw with a start that a green tree frog was clinging to it inches from my face.

When I leaned closer, it jumped about a foot to land at the leaf's center, an impressive performance on the smooth, vertical surface.

There were more spring wildflowers on the hammock floor than I'd thought. Jack-in-the-pulpit, purple false dragonhead, and a delicate white milkweed grew beside swamp rivulets, and wild petunias and white-top sedges hid in grassy glades. The pine scrub was full of flowering shrubs: white bells of rusty lyonia and sparkleberry, yellow tufts of Saint-John's-wort, pink umbels of beautyberry, violet spikes of indigobush. Saw palmettoes bore sprays of waxy little blossoms, and most of the coonties sprouted bulbous female flowers or spiky male ones, although these were hard and dry, the cycads having bloomed in the winter like good tropical plants.

It was late afternoon when I started back. The red light on the new leaves cast watery reflections quite different from the autumn hammock. The air was loaded with a haylike sweetness, a smell particularly strong at the marsh. The rushes and cord grass, which had been flat green and tan in the afternoon sun, now reflected almost lurid colors — magenta, mauve, champagne, powder blue, sparks of vermilion where the sun's light struck directly.

The jade swamp seemed as empty as ever, although the red light made it a warmer emptiness, consommé in a jade bowl. When I walked past the flooded palmetto trunk, however, I glimpsed a swimming motion under the duckweeds, a motion too substantial for a fly or mosquito larva. I waited, but nothing else happened. I gave it up and walked on and saw a similar movement in another duckweed-covered pool. *Something* lived in the jade swamp.

When I got back to the grassy glade where I'd found the tortoise, it was still there. This seemed more startling than the turkeys' utter vanishment. The tortoise looked as though it hadn't moved since I'd first seen it, as though its morning trot had used up its day's supply of energy. It didn't seem distressed, just immobile, hesitating in some lengthy tortoise doubt.

But what could a tortoise doubt? It was unlikely to be lost. Tortoises promptly return to home burrows even when released in unknown territory some distance away. If they can't find a burrow, they can always dig another.

Whatever concerned this tortoise, I didn't seem to concern it anymore. It didn't cringe or run, or even pull into its shell when I passed this time, but just blinked shyly, its nose in the grass.

The Snakes

THE STRANGELY immobile tortoise evoked one of those childhood memories that are so old and dream-like that one wonders if they are real. Before I went to school, my family lived in the Connecticut countryside, and it was a peculiar countryside, in retrospect. Each of the four compass points contained a different world. To the west was a rolling prairie inhabited by bulls and foxes. Indians and Gypsies inhabited cliffs and forests to the north. Eastward was an improbably green river valley, and to the south was a sandy desert inhabited by tortoises.

Tortoises live nowhere near New England in reality. There were other strange things. At the center of these worlds, near the house, was a spring in a grove, and in the spring lived snakes that were at once dangerous and benevolent — guardians. I remembered having a strong sense of these snakes' presence when I passed the spring on the way to the swimming pool into which it flowed. My Grandmother Wallace said that when she went for walks with me around that house, I would insist she not molest any snake we encountered, not even poisonous copperheads. I don't remember this because I couldn't have been more than four at the time, but I still hate to see snakes molested.

My parents were imaginative, well-read people, but their imaginations didn't really extend to snake guardians. There was another presence in the house, however, a woman named Fanny Reeve who had worked for my mother in Virginia and had agreed to come north with us for a while. Fanny Reeve had great-grandchildren: she had been born a slave. She smoked a pipe, wore headcloths, and liked to eat groundhog and pokeweed.

I don't have any very clear memory of Fanny Reeve from that age, of course, but I suspect the rather magical world my sister and I inhabited was largely hers. I have a vague sense of a complex, precise, and appreciative view of landscape. When I visited her in Virginia in later years, she invited me to come see her family's farm in Fluvana County, saying by way of endorsement that there were bears there. It was more than a condescending reference to something that would interest a child. I think she saw it as a good place because there were bears, and I think she would have understood William Bartram's "blue ether of another world."

If the world I inhabited at four was largely Fanny Reeve's, it probably was no accident that tortoises and snake guardians lived there too. The word *gopher* derives from the French for honeycomb, *gaufre de miel,* when it is applied to rodents, but I suspect the etymology is quite different in regard to tortoises. In African mythology, tortoises are the magicians of the animal world. A common word for conjurers among southern blacks in the nineteenth century was *goopher.* Even more prevalent than tortoise magicians in African mythology is the image of a great snake as guardian of the earth. In Dahomeyan mythology, the rainbow serpent Da Aido Hwedo holds together the split gourd of the planet with its multicolored coils.

I wondered if I had stumbled onto some kind of historical

key to Bartram's mysterious vision, if some similar experience had conditioned his unusual respone to landscape. An experience with African mythology is cultural, of course, and I've been talking about culture as a suppressor of innate responses. Yet the continuing power of mythologies might be attributable to their *appeal* to innate mental properties. Indeed, mythologies might be a way of *perpetuating* innate mental responses in the rational, daytime world of culture. With their prehistoric origins and affinity for dreams, mythologies link culture to the unconscious.

There is evidence that Bartram responded imaginatively to African mythology. It's not overt evidence, but that's to be expected, since African culture was more or less taboo in a slaveholding society. Reviewers would probably have called the *Travels* much worse things than "disgustingly pompous" if he'd written about blacks as admiringly as he had about Indians (he got in trouble for that too). But Bartram grew up close to blacks. His father liked them and actually shared his dinner table with his servants, very radical in those days.

Then there was the year at Picolata with six blacks who might have been new arrivals from the middle passage, for all we know. Of course, Bartram was grown up then, less impressionable than a child. Still, the experiences of storekeeping or going bankrupt seem unlikely causes for the magical quality of his perceptions. Other young colonials could have passed a year with six blacks and related to them hardly more than to cattle, but I doubt this of Bartram. Far from striking Simon Legree attitudes, William probably approached his slaveholding career with airy notions of establishing a city of brotherly love in the wilderness, of imbuing his "hands" with Christian ideals. If he was trying to educate them, it could have gone both ways.

The man who threatened his life is interesting. Some of

the most defiant slaves were people of high rank in Africa, priests or other leaders, who considered menial labor beneath their station. The threat doesn't indicate a cordial exchange of views between Bartram and the man, yet the *Travels* shows William had an unusual ability to tolerate hostility and to interest himself in other cultures. His complete silence on Picolata probably arose from shame as well as discretion. Bartram had rather misanthropically high standards of conduct in later life, and his own career as a slaveholder could not have gone well with his principles. It may be significant that his terrified, rapturous encounters on the St. Johns occurred just after he had canoed past his abandoned plantation site. There's an air of release, almost of expiation. "This delightful spot, planted by nature!"

Bartram did refer to tortoises as gophers, and his attitude toward snakes, even poisonous ones, was highly eccentric for colonial America. Benjamin Franklin called rattlesnakes "felons ... convicts from the beginning of the world" and recommended killing them on sight "by virtue of the old law." Bartram referred to the big Florida diamondbacks on more than one occasion as "magnanimous" and "generous" and described at length times when they could have bitten him but didn't. He was reluctant to kill them, felt remorseful when he did, and seems to have half-believed they had the magical power of charming their prey.

Bartram's rattlesnake stories are little myths in themselves. He finds "a cool spring, amidst a grove of the odiferous Myrica; the winding path to this salubrious fountain led through a grassy savanna. I visited the spring several times in the night, but little did I know, or any of my several drowsy companions, that every time we visited the fountain we were in imminent danger ... Early in the morning, excited by unconquerable thirst, I arose and went to the spring; and having, thoughtless of harm or danger, nearly half past the dewy vale, along the serpentine footpath, my hasty steps were suddenly stopped by the sight of a hideous serpent, the formidable rattle-snake, in a high spiral coil, forming a circular mound half the height of my knees, within six inches of the narrow path. As soon as I recovered my senses and strength from so sudden a surprise, I started back out of his reach, where I stood to view him: he lay quiet whilst I surveyed him, appearing no way surprised or disturbed, but kept his half shut eyes fixed on me."

Any interpretations of Bartram's perceptions are likely to remain speculative. Nobody bothered recording much about the response of Africans to the American wilderness. They came from farming, metalworking cultures for the most part, so perhaps they felt as intimidated and alien as most whites did. Yet minds that regard snakes as guardians of the earth might have very different thoughts from those that regard snakes as convicted felons.

Even if African mythology did help open Bartram's mind to Florida, it doesn't prove he had an innate model of a subtropical ecosystem in his brain. Still, this explanation of the Bartram mystery doesn't seem that much stranger than the commonsense one: that William was a sensitive, artistic young man who happened to get thrown into wilderness Florida when a lot of romantic, Rousseauian ideas about nature were in the air. This makes ideas sound like viruses, and if the immune system responds to viruses with innate patterns, who is to say the brain doesn't respond to ideas similarly?

At least the African connection makes a certain evolutionary sense. African myths are not the only ones that feature snake guardians, sacred springs, magic turtles. If these are universal mythical themes, it seems possible that they first evolved in Africa along with the brain and that they retained their purest form in Africa. If Bartram's immune system could carry genetically programmed responses to malarial organisms that his Picolata slaves carried in their blood, why couldn't his brain carry genetically programmed responses to thoughts they carried in their heads? The American fascination with wilderness may not be a new growth, but a loop of the oldest fascination of all.

The Softshell

FLORIDA'S rainy season started soon after I encountered the tortoise, in late May. It was dramatic: a slate blue overcast darkened the west, and a southerly wind drove gray pennants of cloud over the shore at a speed made all the more impressive by the apparent immobility of cumulus banks on the Atlantic horizon.

I watched the sunset at Bulow Creek that evening. In the cold light, the water was gunmetal blue and chrome, and the cord grasses and rushes swayed autumnally over it. A small alligator glided out of the marsh and swam the creek so smoothly it might have been on an underwater track. I wondered how it managed in the current, which seemed pretty strong, the water moving upstream instead of down, pushed by the tide.

I never stopped being impressed by the strength of tidal influence on a creek that was several dozen miles from the nearest ocean inlet, south of Daytona. Within the hammock, about a quarter mile from the creek, was a brackish mudflat. Shorebirds fed on it when it wasn't submerged. Somehow, the tidal water got through the woods into the flat, although there was no sign of a channel, not above ground anyway.

The power of the advancing tidal current caused a startling illusion. It seemed as though something very big was moving up the creek just under the surface, so big that it almost filled the bed. I felt a moment of the vertigo that arises when one stares a long time at running water, then looks at the ground and sees the dry sand or earth appear to eddy and flow.

The rain began as I went to bed that night, at first just a drizzle. A steady pounding on the tile roof awoke me in the small hours. It sounded peremptory, as though the sky was so eager to unload that it had descended to roof level to do it. It continued for twelve hours.

Six inches had fallen by the next afternoon, when the sky lightened, then boiled up into towering thunderheads. The roads looked like canals. A lighter rain kept up for another day, finally thinning to a yellowish overcast that unexpectedly produced window-rattling thunderclaps and twenty minutes of the hardest downpour yet. It flooded my grandmother's yard two inches deep. Her pebbles weren't as absorbent as the neighbors' crabgrass.

The thunderstorm stopped as abruptly as it had started, and I splashed through the flooded roads to the hammock. I didn't expect it to have changed much in a couple of days, but, once again, I hadn't understood it. It hadn't changed in the ways I would have expected. I'd been afraid the sand road would be flooded, since all the paved ones were, but there wasn't even a puddle in it. The sand was firmer than during the dry season: the rain had cemented it.

There wasn't any flooding in the hammock. Swamp rivulets that had dried up during the rainless weeks were full again, but the ones that hadn't dried up seemed no fuller than before. I'd never seen a more graphic demonstration of the spongelike properties of wetland. It was a little eerie. What had the hammock done with all the rain?

Much of it had never even reached the ground. It wasn't that the vegetation had a lot of water on it, in fact it was sur-prisingly dry for less than an hour after a thunderstorm. The vegetation did have a surprising amount of water *in* it that hadn't been there before. The epiphytes, the resurrec-tion ferns and tree mosses that had been mere blackish in-crustations on branches two days before, were now lush, emerald shrouds. Individual resurrection ferns had tripled in size. It was instant rain forest: just add water and stand back.

The downpour had knocked down a few rotted limbs and tattered leaves, but the hammock seemed remarkably un-disturbed. Mosquitoes and flies were less in evidence, but birds and frogs called lustily in the canopy, and life seemed encouraged rather than intimidated. A barred owl flew out of a thicket and landed on a branch in full view, behavior I'd seen in the Okefenokee but not the hammock.

A large brown frog sitting on a snag in a swamp rivulet also demurred to flee at my approach. I wondered if it was the ranid species that I'd heard calling at night. It might have been a bronze frog: the distant chorus had had a clacking sound heard among that species. On the other hand, it might have been a southern leopard frog, since its snout had a characteristic shape, or a pickerel frog, since its legs had yellow patches. The frog just sat there, as though daring me to come and attempt identification. Even herpetologists have trouble sorting out southern frogs.

An armadillo rummaged in the leaf litter, also ignoring me, although the sun hadn't set. It thrust its head under the leaves, pushed its whole body into a tree hole, rose like a bear on hind legs to tear at a stump. The sound of its own scratchings seemed to startle it: it suddenly jumped sideways. Then it stuck its head back into the ground.

When I got to the ditch, a songbird was scolding in a tangle of vines. Another barred owl flew out of it and landed in the open. It was facing away from me, but turned its head around 180 degrees to stare. Yet another started calling to the south.

I came to the place in the sand pine scrub where I thought I'd heard frogs in the night. Since it wasn't getting dark yet, I left the path and pushed through the saw palmetto. In a little while, I saw an opening in the brush and started toward it. I wasn't expecting much, a scattering of brackish puddles and rivulets as in other swampy parts of the hammock. I'd misunderstood it again.

I found myself on the edge of a sizeable sheet of water that was translucent black, like obsidian, quite unlike the brown murky water of the brackish tidal swamps. It stretched out of sight eastward. Around it, and in its shallows, grew some of the biggest trees I'd seen in the hammock, not only palmettoes and red cedars, but great, buttressed American elms, swamp hickories, Carolina ashes, and gums. Buttonbushes grew farther out in the water, tall shrubs bearing masses of spherical white flowers, and a clump of willows stood in the sunny center.

It was a sweetwater swamp, isolated from the tides by slightly higher land, and fed by some intricacy of limestone aquifer, some vagrant but copious outlier of Bartram's "salubrious fountains." It glowed in its scrubby setting, the new hardwood leaves reflected in water already green with duckweed, aquatic *Salvinia* ferns and lotuslike floating hearts. Even underwater, the swamp was full of green plants, feathery-leaved bladderworts and stoneworts. The presence of carnivorous bladderworts indicated that it was also full of the water fleas and other zooplankton I missed in the jade swamp.

I walked along the water's edge, expecting to come to the end of it pretty soon, since the creek was in that direction. Yet it kept stretching ahead of me, and it was so different from anything I'd seen in the hammock before that it began to seem unreal. I felt dislocated, as I had felt when trying to follow the path in the dark, although this time it was exhilarating instead of intimidating.

I skirted a palmetto trunk and almost stumbled over a spray of green stems on its base. It was a whisk fern, a very healthy one. I found another of the ancient plants a few yards further, growing on the base of another palmetto along with a little moss garden of liverworts, maiden cane, and red cedar seedlings. I wondered what whisk ferns had grown on the bases of before palmettoes evolved.

I glimpsed something in flight and heard a furtive splash, then a wood duck drake was swimming among the buttonbushes, making peevish sounds. He climbed on a log and peered at me through the foliage. The red skin around his eye gave him an intense stare even at a distance. As I stood still, not wanting to frighten the duck, I noticed other creatures: a brown frog like the one I'd seen earlier, except that this one still had its tail, and a big black cooter turtle. The turtle had its neck craned anxiously, watching me. When I glanced away a moment, it slipped into the water so quietly I was unsure I'd ever seen it. When I looked back at the wood duck, it had disappeared too.

A live oak had fallen in the water, forming a natural boardwalk. I climbed out over its slippery carpet of epiphytes and sat where the main limbs branched from the trunk. The reddening sky intensified the treetops' reflections in the swamp, but its water was so clear I could still see the bottom easily. Even the mosquito fish in it seemed larger and more colorful than those in the brackish swamps. Many of the large females had swollen bellies: more mosquito fish on the way.

I glimpsed a movement at the surface out of the corner of my eye. When I turned to look, I could see nothing but water plants and floating twigs, but I was getting impatient with all these vanishing acts. The spot was about eight feet away, far enough to focus my binoculars on. I did, and saw with a start that there was an eye down there at the surface. Apparently it was unconnected to anything else, like the Cheshire cat's smile. It wasn't the black, impassive eye of a frog or cooter turtle. This eye had a sharpness about it. It was yellow like a cat's, and it kept blinking nervously. When I leaned forward to see it better, the eye disappeared as though the swamp itself had shut it, as though other eyes might start appearing on tree trunks or sandbars.

I waited, keeping my binoculars on the spot. Then the eye was there again. I noticed a dot in front of it. A nostril? I leaned forward again, and as the eye vanished again, I glimpsed a snaky motion underwater, as of a neck being withdrawn.

When the eye reappeared, I knew what it belonged to. A softshell turtle was buried in the waterweeds and fallen leaves, its long neck extended to the surface with only eyes and nostrils protruding. Surface reflection concealed the rest of its strangely beaked and flattened head. To disappear, it had withdrawn head and neck so smoothly that my eye hadn't caught the movement.

I remembered watching softshells in the Olentangy River in Columbus, Ohio, sticking their birdlike heads out of the water as rush hour traffic roared past on riverfront freeways. In wooded areas upstream from town, they'd climb out to bask on the bank a few feet from me if I remained still, but at the slightest movement they'd drop into the water faster than the eye could follow. Softshells can move fast enough to catch trout. They had seemed fabulously unturtlelike, more like little shield-bearing dragons with their flat, leathery shells and catlike eyes. Bartram was fascinated by Florida softshells and devoted two copper plates in the *Travels* to drawings of them as well as describing them in the text, as though to convince himself that this creature truly existed. One of his drawings is so strange-looking that it takes a while to figure out that it is a turtle's head and not some strange mollusk or crustacean.

This turtle evidently thought it had me fooled. It seemed prepared to trade blinks with me indefinitely, but darkness was falling, and I hadn't brought a flashlight. I got off the log and started back toward the path.

Frogs had started calling somewhere, I couldn't tell where. They might have been in the water right beside me, for all I knew, or in my head. The high-pitched trilling, unlike any call I'd heard in the hammock before, was so loud that it seemed to obliterate any sense of direction. It rose to a crescendo that made my ears ring, then stopped suddenly.

It might have seemed ominous, especially after finding the apparently disembodied eye. But coming upon the softshell somehow had evoked the same unaccountable happiness as stumbling on the copulating stinkpots. The thunder-cleared air seemed vinous again, although lighter than the November air had been, a Chardonnay instead of a Beaujolais. Although the sunlight was gone from the woods, they appeared shadowless.

When I got to the marsh, I smelled a sweet, acrid fragrance that seemed familiar, although I'd never smelled it in the hammock. It reminded me of sleeping on the porch of my mother's parents' house in Virginia when I'd visited them in summer as a child. Looking around for the source, I noticed drifts of tiny, white, four-petaled flowers on the path. Sprays of the flowers covered some small evergreen trees, and the smell was coming from them, which didn't explain anything, since the trees were dahoon trees, a species that doesn't grow in Virginia.

The luminous dusk and strangely familiar fragrance made the hammock seem more confiding than it ever had before. Even the jade swamp finally gave up its secrets—at least, I discovered what lived in the flooded palmetto stump besides fly and mosquito larvae. As I passed it this time, a small toad floated calmly on its surface, wearing a duckweed hat. It didn't dive out of sight as I approached, or even when I touched it. It perhaps was too excited about the opening of its breeding season to pay attention to me. I met more of them along the path, little buffy toads with red warts—oak toads. I'd never seen one before in the hammock.

The darkness didn't evoke any of the unease it had on previous occasions. Frog and insect calls sounded less furtive, and the fireflies' light had a robustness, an orange lustre, which seemed new. The sky glowed even after the last red had faded. Drops of water on fallen leaves reflected the glow in little flashes as I passed them, and the hammock seemed full of silver lights beneath the fireflies' golden ones.

Common Sense

I REALIZED later why the dahoon trees' fragrance beside the marsh had reminded me of my grandparents' house. Some big English holly trees that my grandparents had brought from Oregon had lived under the sleeping porch. Dahoon and holly belong to the same genus, *Ilex*, and the dahoon smell evidently had been enough like holly to evoke my memories of it.

The association made me notice something. I had stopped smelling the spicy, seductive, dangerous smell that had struck me when I'd first gone to the hammock, and then when I'd returned to it after many years. I couldn't even recall what the smell had been, because the brain can't seem to "visualize" past smells as it can sights or sounds. Instead of that one powerful smell of exotic promise and warning, the hammock now contained hundreds of smells, many of them quite familiar.

It was strange to have such a strong element of the past simply dissolve. The retention of memory is a basic component of rational consciousness, but here was a memory that could not be retained, that slipped away almost imperceptibly into a part of the brain I couldn't control, couldn't even really locate. It was as though my impression of the hammock had gotten lost in the hammock, my original strong sensations so worn through in daily contact, so tangled in thousands of new sensations, as to be reduced to a kind of quotidian oblivion.

In a way it seemed to confirm the common sense that organisms and not ecosystems are the highest living entities. As the hammock was a loose assemblage of plants and animals, my perception of it seemed to have dissolved into a loose assemblage of miscellaneous sights, sounds, and smells, their diversity obliterating any original impression of significant relationship, any inkling of innate response. Certainly, the hammock did not seem to relate to me as another organism would have. It seemed indifferent to my comings and goings.

Except, of course, that it *didn't* really seem indifferent to my comings and goings. It was full of moods—frightening, welcoming, fragrant, uncomfortable—it was just that, as a commonsense organism, I considerd them *my* moods. But what if I was less integral than I thought? What if parts of my brain had their own hidden relationships with environment? Whose moods were they then? Whose original impression had it been?

In fact, my experience in the hammock had not increased my confidence in being a commonsense organism. When my original impression dissolved into diversity, it had not only made the hammock seem random and unconnected, it had made my own consciousness seem random and unconnected. Further, I had often felt that this randomness and unconnectedness was superficial, a confusion obscuring relationships of which I had only the vaguest comprehension or even awareness.

For example, although it seemed that my experience of the hammock simply rode off in a thousand random directions, it didn't really. It underwent a rather steady rhythm of expansion and contraction that reminded me of heart-beat or breathing. The expansion of my first enthralled perception of the hammock preceded the contraction of my first uneasy realization of its secretiveness, and so on up to the most recent expansion of discovering the sweetwater swamp. Although my wanderings in the hammock appeared random, they assumed a shape in my mind like a series of caves, each with a dark entrance leading into a lighted interior that had at its farthest recess another dark entrance. Much as Florida has changed, it was very like the savanna grove, spring, grotto pattern of Bartram's wanderings. Common sense told me that Bulow Hammock was a tattered, inconsequential remnant of departed glory; experience seemed to tell me that I could go wandering around in it indefinitely and somehow not come to the end of it.

Of course, this eternal wandering was what Audubon's lost one was afraid of. But perhaps that fear depends on the commonsense belief that ecosystems aren't entities. If they are entities with which we have innate relationships, wandering in them is not a form of banishment but a kind of acquaintanceship. I did feel I got to know the hammock better each time I entered one of its "caverns," and not only in a geographical or scientific sense. What I learned about geography or biology simply confirmed previous knowledge, but I became acquainted with other things that I was much less equipped to interpret, but which seemed no less interesting for that.

Why had my brain seemed to light up each time I encountered a turtle in the mud? It's easy to account for the mental contortions humans tend to undergo with snakes. Snakes can kill you, and they have fairly obvious sexual connotations. But why this unaccountable sense of happiness about a two-hundred-million-year-old reptile sandwiched between plates of bone? African myths are impressed with tortoises' ability to resemble stones by pulling into their shells. Perhaps turtles are associated with the emergence of life from stony matter, as when the planet itself is seen as riding on a turtle's back. Turtles and tortoises may have been among the more useful food sources for early hominids. Perhaps they seemed helpful emissaries between the stony and soft sides of existence, magically turning rocks into meat.

Such speculations are crude and unverifiable. Yet if the brain is not a tabula rasa but a storehouse of genetically coded information about the environment as well as the organism, as it may be, there's likely to be something about turtles in there quite apart from what we've learned about them culturally. When I seemed to find turtles at the places where the hammock contracted into darkness before opening again into light, it may not have been entirely accidental. Certainly, my experience of turtles in the hammock didn't confirm commonsense notions of them as dull and plodding.

The Otter

 MY ATTEMPT to repeat the Bulow Hammock experiment seemed modestly successful. I'd not only found
alligators, but I'd found turkeys and tortoises, the whole program the ranger had announced, not to mention softshell
turtles in swamps and toads in stumps.

I wasn't sure what use it all was, aside from providing me
some perhaps temporary sense that by finding these things
I'd found parts of myself, not just the cultural parts, but little-
known, innate ones. At least, repeating the experiment had
been useful in demonstrating that it could be repeated. Evolution and life can be seen as experiments, with success reward-
ed by the opportunity for further experiment.

I visited the hammock again in early January of 1987. There
had been forest fires on the coast in 1985, and I was afraid
of finding a blackened ruin. Hammocks aren't fire-adapted
ecosystems as southern pinelands and prairies are. I found,
however, that the fire had stopped at the pine woods just to
the north. The hammock's sponginess seemed to make it as
impervious to fire as it was to flood. A scattering of charred
pines and palmettoes on the marsh horizon was the only
vestige of the destruction.

The hammock was drier than I'd ever seen it, despite persistent rain the day before. A depression near the trailhead that had always been a deep puddle wasn't even muddy, and the swamp rivulets were very low. The dryness hadn't stopped the hammock's fungus populations from responding exuberantly to the rain. There'd never been so many mushrooms: big, pearly amanitas, some with yellow warts; red-topped russulas; clumps of smallish golden armillarias. Velvety ochre bracket fungi grew out of saw palmetto roots. Chestnut brown brackets covered dead cabbage palmetto roots.

Here, it seemed, was yet another case of organs relating independently to environment while the organism took a back seat, but this was an even more flagrant case than brains or flowers. Mushrooms are merely the reproductive organs of fungi, but they are so much more specialized, colorful, and elaborate than the amorphous, threadlike hyphae that comprise the main organism as to appear the fungus's raison d'être rather than vice versa. Mushrooms busily attract and repel animals like flies and humans with smells, shapes, and chemistry, while their hyphae just sit there in the ground. That such "wayward" organs could have evolved at the "primitive" fungal level, as well as at the seed, plant, and hominid levels, again suggested some kind of basic tendency for such evolution.

Many of the fungi that brandished extravagant mushrooms about the hammock had stopped being organisms in the true sense. Their specialized hyphal cells, mycorrhizae, had become organs of the trees, in effect. They had replaced the root cells of most of the hammock's tree species in the function of drawing water and nutrients from the soil, taking food from the trees' sap in exchange. Thus, their mushrooms had become part of the flowers in the canopy, each attracting spore-eating flies or beetles, or pollen-eating bees or flies to perpetuate a superorganism, a forest. If mushrooms and flowers were linked in this subtle way, it made me wonder where brains might fit in. I could think of at least one way: the acorn-hiding brains of birds and squirrels also perpetuate the forest.

Aside from the mushrooms, the hammock seemed a little shrunken and dull in its dryness. Dessicated epiphytes littered the ground. A pileated woodpecker squawked peevishly somewhere, and as I approached, an armadillo sat up and sniffed nearsightedly, pink snout twitching. The only plants that had grown noticeably were the canes in the glades, which now stood over my head.

The sinkhole where I'd found the stinkpots copulating was almost dry. The only sign of turtles was an abandoned-looking gopher tortoise hole in the bank. The sweetwater swamp where I'd found the softshell was even drier, and willows had grown and spread to obscure the vista that had impressed me three years before. Once mysteriously luminescent with its sheet of obsidian water, the dried swamp seemed disheveled and deserted, hardly the same place, and I wasn't altogether sure it was, although the location seemed right.

I still had hopes for alligators on Bulow Creek. It was the right time of year, right weather. I pushed through the brush on the north side of the drainage ditch until I reached the red cedar and baccharis along the creek, but the view wasn't any better than it had been in April. I heard some birds flying away, and glimpsed a lone green heron, but I was too far upstream to see the mudbank where the alligators might be sunning.

I decided to wade the ditch. It was still full of water, but the sand bottom seemed firm. The cold water made my legs ache, but I got across without getting wetter than that. I followed the ditch east to the mound from which I'd watched the alligators five years before. My caution in peeking over the mound was wasted. The tide was high. Not only did I see no alligators, but I saw no mudbank, just water and saw grass. Even the green heron had disappeared.

I returned to my ford, waded back across, and lay down in the sun to dry off. Vultures circled overhead: I tried to see if they were blacks or turkeys. Then I heard something from the ditch a few yards away and looked up. An otter had surfaced in the water near where I'd climbed out on the other bank. It was growling at me, a small, irascible sound. Then it turned and began swimming upstream.

I'd noticed an underwater burrow entrance in the bank there. It seemed I'd disturbed the otter's afternoon nap in its den by clambering over the roof. I could understand its annoyance, especially when it emerged to find a stranger sprawled across its doorstep.

I watched the V of its wake receding up the ditch, supposing that would be the last I'd see of it. Then the otter did an unexpected thing. When it was a couple of hundred feet away, it suddenly turned and swam back. A few dozen feet upstream of me, it dived, but I could see its continued downstream course by a trail of bubbles. The bubbles came abreast of the burrow entrance and stopped. The otter surfaced, looked me straight in the face, growled again, then swam toward the burrow entrance, dived, and disappeared, evidently back to its interrupted nap.

I felt I understood perfectly what had gone on in the otter's head. It was what would have gone on in mine if I'd been disturbed in my residence by a noisy clod, had started to flee to quieter surroundings, then had gotten righteously indignant at the imposition and gone back to reclaim my rightful place.

I couldn't recall a more convincing display of conscious volition in a wild animal. When the sunbathing alligators had fled into the water after I appeared on the mound above Bulow Creek, they had certainly shown consciousness, but there'd been an element of automatism in their prompt reappearance on the bank when I'd kept still. The reappearance seemed motivated as much by short attention spans as by a determination to keep sunbathing. The turkey hens that had returned to get their chicks had certainly shown volition, but there'd been a strong instinctual element in their concern for their young. In contrast, the otter's refusal to be driven from its den seemed entirely personal, willful. Its awareness of my presence had never wavered, yet it had come back anyway. Its irritable attachment to its own space and comfort suggested a sense of self like my own.

It was strange to think of such a consciousness inhabiting the hammock full-time. We tend to think of personality and selfhood as cultural rather than natural, but here was a creature living in a hole in the bank who seemed as individuated as my neighbors in Ormond Beach. It implied that the individual integrity we feel as organisms is not something that emerges from ecosystems, but something that fits *in* them.

Yet how can something that seems as separate as individual consciousness fit into something that seems as indifferent as an ecosystem? If the brain is the organism's survival computer, perhaps it can't fit for very long. If the brain is a semi-independent mediator between organism and ecosystem, however, the idea of a fit between the two makes more sense. If the brain is a mediator, then consciousness is not really separate.

Such ideas may seem mystical, but we know so little about the relationship of consciousness and life that they can't justly be discarded. We live daily with unanswered questions which make the "abominable mystery" of flowering plant origins seem fit for elementary school. I passed one on the way out of the hammock. I turned over a log and found a dark brown anole under it.

I wondered how the anole had managed to match the color of the leaf mold under the log when, presumably, there had been no light under the log and thus no color. But that wasn't the main question, which remained as to how the lizard's brain was able to assimilate information about the color of the environment and program it back into the color of its skin. We know the mechanism for the skin's color change — pigment cells — but not for the basic transferral of information.

The hammock was very still as I walked out. This should have allowed me to remember that I'd wanted to see if I'd smell the old seductive, dangerous smell again after being away for three years. I didn't think of it until I was bumping away down the sand road. I realized that I probably hadn't smelled it if I hadn't even remembered to see if I smelled it, but I stopped the car and opened the window anyway. I sniffed. The January air smelled only faintly of sand and spice and not at all of 1950s cocktail lounges. The green tunnel looked as seductive and impenetrable as ever, though. I felt little more certainty about what lay inside it than I had in 1953.

Bibliography

Andrews, Henry N. *Studies in Paleobotany.* New York: Wiley, 1961.

Arnold, Chester A. *An Introduction to Paleobotany.* New York: McGraw-Hill, 1947.

Audubon, John James. *Ornithological Biography.* Edinburgh, Scotland: A. Black, 1839.

Baker, Mary Francis. *Florida Wild Flowers.* New York: Macmillan, 1949.

Barbour, Thomas. *That Vanishing Eden: A Naturalist's Florida.* Boston: Little Brown, 1945.

Bartram, William. *Travels Through North and South Carolina, Georgia, East and West Florida, The Cherokee Country, The Extensive Territories of the Muscogulges, or Creek Confederacy, and the Country of the Chactaws.* Philadelphia: James and Johnson, 1791.

Beck, Charles B. (editor). *Origin and Early Evolution of Angiosperms.* New York and London: Columbia University Press, 1976.

Berrill, N. J. *Man's Emerging Mind.* New York: Dodd, Mead, 1955.

Berry, Edward Wilber. *Tree Ancestors.* Baltimore: Williams & Watkins, 1923.

Cabell, James Branch, and A.J Hanna. *The St. Johns: A Parade of Diversities.* New York: Farrar & Rinehart, 1943.

Carr, Archie. *Handbook of Turtles.* Ithaca, N.Y.: Cornell University Press, 1952.

Conant, Roger. *A Field Guide to Reptiles and Amphibians of Eastern and Central North America.* Boston: Houghton Mifflin, 1975.

Coon, Carleton S. *The Origin of Races.* New York: Knopf, 1963.

Corner, E. J. H. "The Evolution of Tropical Forest." In *Evolution as a Process,* Julian S. Huxley (editor). London: George Allen & Unwin, 1945.

————. *The Natural History of Palms.* Berkeley and Los Angeles: University of California Press, 1966.

Darrah, William C. *Principles of Paleobotany.* New York: Ronald, 1960.

Dasmann, Raymond F. *No Further Retreat: The Fight to Save Florida.* New York: Macmillan, 1971.

Dormon, Caroline. *Flowers Native to the Deep South.* Baton Rouge, La.: Claitor's Book Store, 1958.

Durant, Mary, and Michael Harwood. *On the Road with John James Audubon.* New York: Dodd, Mead, 1980.

Earnest, Ernest. *John and William Bartram: Botanists and Explorers.* Philadelphia: University of Pennsylvania Press, 1940.

Eisley, Loren. *The Firmament of Time.* New York: Atheneum, 1960.

Ellenberger, Henri E. *The Discovery of the Unconscious.* New York: Basic Books, 1970.

Ernst, Carl H., and Roger W. Barbour. *Turtles of the United States.* Lexington: University Press of Kentucky, 1972.

Forsyth, Adrian, and Ken Miyata. *Tropical Nature.* New York: Scribner's, 1984.

Gould, Stephen Jay. *Hen's Teeth and Horse's Toes: Further Reflections in Natural History.* New York: Norton, 1983.

————. *The Mismeasure of Man.* New York: Norton, 1981.

Grimm, William Carey. *Recognizing Native Shrubs.* Harrisburg, Pa.: Stackpole (no date).

Helfer, Jacques R. *How to Know the Grasshoppers, Cockroaches and Their Allies.* Dubuque, Ia.: Wm. C. Brown Company, 1963.

Herbst, Josephine. *New Green World.* New York: Hastings House, 1954.

Howell, F. Clark, and Francois Bourliere (editors). *African Ecology and Human Evolution.* Chicago: Aldine, 1963.

Hughes, Norman F. *Paleobiology of Angiosperm Origins.* Cambridge, England: Cambridge University Press, 1976.

Hume, H. Harold. *Hollies.* New York: Macmillan, 1953.

Hutchins, Ross E. *Island of Adventure: A Naturalist Explores a Gulf Coast Wilderness.* New York: Dodd, Mead, 1968.

Johanson, Donald. *Lucy: The Beginnings of Humankind.* New York: Simon & Schuster, 1981.

Kastner, Joseph. *A Species of Eternity.* New York: Knopf, 1977.

Keating, Edward M. *The Broken Bough: A Solution to the Riddle of Man.* New York: Atheneum, 1975.

Kurten, Bjorn. *The Age of Mammals.* New York and London: Columbia University Press, 1971.

Kurz, Herman, and Robert K. Godrey. *Trees of Northern Florida.* Gainesville: University of Florida Press, 1962.

Lakela, Olga, and Robert W. Long. *Ferns of the Southeastern States.* Miami: Banyan Books, 1976.

Leakey, Richard E., and Roger Lewin. *Origins.* New York: Dutton, 1977.

Ley, Willy. *Dragons in Amber.* New York: Viking, 1951.

Linné, Sir Charles (Linnaeus). *A General System of Nature Through the Three Grand Kingdoms.* London: Lackington, Allen, and Company, 1806.

Lowenstein, Jerold M. "The Search for a Human Ancestor," *Pacific Discovery,* January-March 1984.

Marais, Eugene. *The Soul of the Ape.* New York: Atheneum, 1969.

Mayr, Ernst (editor). *The Species Problem.* Washington, D.C.: Publication No. 50, American Association for the Advancement of Science, 1957.

McLoughlin, John C. *Synapsida: A New Look into the Origin of Mammals.* New York: Viking, 1980.

Montagu, Ashley. *Man's Most Dangerous Myth: The Fallacy of Race.* New York and London: Columbia University Press, 1945.

Muir, John. *A Thousand Mile Walk to the Gulf.* Boston: Houghton Mifflin, 1916.

Neill, Wilfred T. *The Geography of Life.* New York and London: Columbia University Press, 1969.

Olson, Everett C. *Vertebrate Paleozoology.* New York: Wiley, 1971.

Pfeiffer, John E. *The Emergence of Man.* New York: Harper & Row, 1969.

Pilbeam, David. "The Descent of Hominoids and Hominids," *Scientific American,* March 1984.

Proby, Kathryn Hall. *Audubon in Florida: With Selections from the Writings of John James Audubon.* Coral Gables, Fla.: University of Miami Press, 1974.

Shelford, Victor Earnest. *Ecology of North America.* Urbana: University of Illinois Press, 1963.

Simpson, Charles Torrey. *Florida Wild Life.* New York: Macmillan, 1932.

———. *In Lower Florida Wilds.* New York: Putnam, 1920.

_____. *Out of Doors in Florida.* Miami: E. B. Douglas, 1923.

Small, John Kunkell. *Ferns of the Southeastern States.* New York: Hafner, 1964.

Stirton, R. A. *Time, Life, and Man.* New York: Wiley, 1959.

Taylor, Gordon Rattray. *The Great Evolution Mystery.* New York: Harper & Row, 1983.

Turnbull, Colin. *Man in Africa.* Garden City, N.Y.: Anchor Press/Doubleday, 1976.

U.S. Fish and Wildlife Service. *Coastal Ecosystems of the Southeastern United States: Proceedings of U.S. Fish and Wildlife Service Workshop, Coastal Ecosystems Project.* Washington, D.C.: U.S. Department of Interior (no date).

Wendt, Herbert. *Before the Deluge.* Garden City, N.Y.: Doubleday, 1968.

Wilson, Ruth Danehower. "The Bulow Plantation of 1821–1835," *The Florida Historical Quarterly,* April 1945.